THE DAY I WON

£117,998,147.47

JAMES PARSONS

First published in paperback by
Michael Terence Publishing in 2022
www.mtp.agency

ISBN 9781800944428

Michael Terence
Publishing

Thank you for purchasing this book and I hope you enjoy reading it as much as I did writing it. If you are so lucky as to win a large amount of money, please feel free to use this book as a template to progress your success as for me it was a dream of fiction, for you, it could be reality.

- James Parsons

1

The beginning

It was Sunday, January 27th 2007 and I had forgotten to check my lotto numbers as normal. I had been at work all day and it never entered my mind to look to see if I had won anything. I bought the ticket three days before from the corner shop when I went to get a bottle of wine to have with our dinner on the forthcoming Sunday. My daughter Danielle and future son-in-law Jake came around on Sunday to have Sunday lunch with us as was normal and it was after dinner that sitting in the living-room watching TV and chatting, I decided to check my ticket.

Let us start at the beginning, I was born in Plymouth in 1955 to my mother, Joy, and my father, Jim, and when I was seven, we moved to the Midlands because my father and been offered a promotion to Head of Department/Deputy Head. My father was in many ways a wise man, as being a teacher, he had quite a lot of time free to pursue other things. One of these was purchasing old run-down properties and doing them up. When I was thirteen, I became the labour, mixing concrete, holding one thing or the other. At one stage he had fourteen properties on the go, most rented out and it seemed, that there was always work to be done on one of them. I did not do well at school in any subject apart from rural science, but I somehow managed to get top of the school as this was the only subject that interested me. I wanted to become a landscape gardener when I left school but knew that I would have to have some good grounding and qualifications behind me, this with my poor school results would be difficult.

I applied for a job at fourteen at Walsall Arboretum and to my surprise was offered a position as a trainee in the arboretum nursery; I would have to do five years of training and should I prove myself any good, I would be offered a position as an apprentice for a further five years. My salary would be £5 per week paid weekly subject to the normal taxes etc. Being a trainee/apprentice for a total of ten years played on my mind as at fourteen it seemed like a very, very long way away. With this in my mind, I decided to look at joining the Army. I discussed this with my parents and made some tentative enquiries. It was at this point I discovered that I would be required to take an exam. Having kept it secret from everyone, I had to tell my parents that I could not read. To my surprise my parents did not hit the roof, I imagine my father must have felt a little ashamed that he had not realised.

The following day my father came home with the old-fashioned books called 'Janet and John', these were books for beginners to learn the basics and for my father to establish what level I was at. I had a few months to learn to read before I had to go to the Army recruitment centre to take my exam. On completion, I was offered, two positions, one being Infantry at Wittington Barracks by Lichfield and the other was Army Apprentice College, Pirbright. I decided on the local one at Lichfield. When I arrived at Lichfield on September 1st 1970, I was asked if I was interested in playing a musical instrument, as my father had been in the R.A.F. and was quite musical I thought this would please him and as I was told I would be able to do all the other types of things like shoot guns and do plenty of running around, I jumped at the chance. To my disappointment, I spent months sitting in a room trying to play my flute having no one to show me how to go about it as the band did not have anyone competent or interested in the flute to show me.

Some fifteen months later having been promoted to Lance Corporal - I don't know how - I decided to ask to be transferred. One week later I was an Infantryman; they let me keep my Lance Corporal's strip. With all the running around and learning about weapons, I felt exonerated in my decision to transfer. During my two years as a junior soldier, I participated in many sports, including boxing, athletics, judo, cross country and rugby and loved them all. I had won company colours several times and added many cups and trophies to my collection. During my time as a junior soldier, I had been promoted to full Corporal, however, once you had to leave juniors, this promotion became invalid.

Then came the big day for me to go into man's service. Fortunately, the transfer was conducted at the same barracks in Lichfield, that was in October 1972. Normal basic training for new recruits lasted fourteen weeks and as I had many of the basics, I entered at eight weeks into the programme. The intake was large by normal standards and this had been increased by having thirty ex-juniors bolstering the numbers. Within a few days, the powers that be decided not to allow the ex-juniors to be eligible for the standard awards: shooting; best dressed; fittest; marching, etc and they introduced a special award for the best ex-junior as the intake had been so large and they did not want the ex-juniors taking the awards from the new recruits.

I was in the running for the award until our final exercise in Wales. I had been picked to play the part of an enemy soldier. All went smoothly during the exercises and I knew I had done well until the last, long twenty-five miles march in full gear and weapons. I developed a blood blister on the ball of my foot due to stepping on a bottle the year before in bare feet very drunk. I got into bed and it was only when a mate of mine noticed blood dripping through my mattress, that they carried me over to the medical centre. The M.O, who appeared to be of retirement age, decided to stitch me up. The only anaesthetic available was seven years old and should have been disposed of after one year.

With three chaps holding me down the doc went to work. I was very sober by the time he had finished. Anyway, I digress, at some point, a small fragment of glass must have been left behind and this had caused the ball of my foot to go very swollen and green. I was transported back to Lichfield where it was sorted, but I felt hugely disappointed having blown my chances of getting the coveted award of Best Ex-junior. Then to my complete surprise, I still won!

Having passed out of basic training, I went on leave back home for Christmas and was due to report for duty on the 1st of January 1973, with my regiment the 1st Staffordshire stationed in Dover. On my way to reporting, I was involved in a road traffic accident; a car pulled out in front of my motorcycle smashing my leg and causing a nasty laceration. I was carted off to the local hospital and they promptly put me into a cast and settled me down for the night. The next day the Army came for me and transferred me to RAF Cosford military hospital. They swiftly removed the cast, grumbling all the time that it was not done properly.

I spent seventeen days at Cosford and must say I had great fun with the nurses. I did manage to get through five plaster casts during my stay and this was mainly messing around and cracking them. On release from hospital, I was sent home for three months, having been so active it felt like a prison sentence. After three months and with my plaster removed, I was ordered back to Lichfield. I was told that I would remain at Lichfield until my leg was working properly and then sent on to my regiment. The trouble was they did not know what to do with me. They decided to make me the Regimental Sergeant Major's Batman for the duration, working out of the guard room. Polishing his boots and Sam Brown, I did manage to get a lucrative thing going, bulling up the boots of the new recruits - at a cost, of course.

Finally, I was given my chance to join the battalion. I travelled down to Dover with a couple of other chaps who were also due to join the Staffords. On arrival, we were paraded in front of the Company Sergeant Major. He noticed I had my marksman badge and commented this would put me in good stead. I was still limping a fair bit and struggling to keep up with training on miles of marches with full equipment and weapons. I soon got up to standard and after six months, got promoted to Lance Corporal to the disagreement of many of what are called 'old sweats' who felt that no one should be promoted until they'd spent a couple of years with the battalion.

Within a few months of joining my regiment, we were deployed to Londonderry, Northern Ireland. This was a four-month-posting working seven days a week until at some time you were allowed four days rest and recuperation. While I was at Londonderry a pal gave me a girl's address and I started writing to her on my Rest and Recuperation. We met up and had a wonderful time visiting the nightclubs and pubs in Birmingham. After my tour of Ireland, we returned to Dover and I was sent on leave over the Christmas period. We again had the best of times enjoying the nightlife that any young couple in love could find.

After only being together for a short period, I knew that

this was the girl I wanted to spend the rest of my life with and we decided to get engaged. We were married six months later at 11.40 am on the 7th of June in the West Bromwich registry office and honeymooned in Torquay, Devon. I enjoyed my time in the Army and was promoted twice in only a few years, but my heart had gone out of it and on the 29th of June 1978 I finally managed to purchase my release from the Army. The last year of my service in the armed forces was possibly the best and the worst. On July 7th, 1977 Guatemala was threatening to invade Belize. We were point battalion for the British Army and therefore on twenty-four hours standby for any reason we may have been called upon. Within twenty-four hours, we were starting our descent to the airport of Belize city airport; one runway with anti-aircraft batteries on each side following in our aircraft as we landed. The doors to the aircraft opened and the heat hit you like a furnace. At the side of the runway, a group of soldiers were using pickaxes and shovels to do some work, just watching them, you felt drained.

Our first three weeks were spent acclimatising to the heat and doing lots of running to force our speedy acclimatisation. During this time, I had been acting as Platoon Sergeant and this continued once we were deployed into the jungle with half the platoon. As we were the first troops to be deployed since the potential hostilities had been declared, we had our training conducted by the S.A.S. who had been in theatre for some weeks. This was what we as soldiers had trained for all our soldiering lives. Training was hard, wet and sticky, but I must admit, I loved it. Once our heroes had left us to it, we were deployed by chopper into the dense jungle to act as a slowing down of Guatemalan troops if they decided to invade.

We quickly learnt how to and how not to move through

the jungle. Every day we would see sights that I found fascinating. Large iguanas often six feet or more; snakes of various sizes were a regular concern as we would see at least ten a day. We saw hummingbirds, frogs the size of rabbits and ants of all types, I found the whole experience a wonder and the height of my career. Towards the end of our almost six months, a Welsh regiment came out to relieve us. By now the hostilities had been pushed into the background. After a couple of months, most of it spent in the jungle, I was informed that my daughter had been born some seventeen days prior to my finding out. My first beautiful baby girl, Donna, was born on the 10th of August 1977 weighing in at 8 pounds and 7 ounces.

Just before our return, the Welsh regiment replacing us was sent in to test our abilities. Needless to say, they advanced at company strength and would have been wiped out within the first half mile of advance. Our tactic and training had paid off. We returned to the UK at the end of November only to be put onto firefighting as the fire brigade was having some sort of fallout over salaries. I was shipped off to a place called Oakham in Leicestershire for three and a half months as commander of the detachment. It was a fun period; one day we were called out to an old boy's house that had a chimney fire, while working out what to do, you should stick the hosepipe up the chimney or down from the roof. Luckily, a fire officer not on strike came along and showed us what to do. Rack the fire low, put a tray or small spade on the glowing embers and sprinkle water onto it, the steam puts the fire out. Simple when you know how.

All the time this was going on, troops were marching through the house with hosepipes and trying to figure it out, this old boy was sitting in the kitchen eating his meal on wheels, never looked up, never said a word. Gratitude for you; having said that, we could have flooded his home. It had taken me eighteen months to get out of the Army and this decision had been made on the following grounds. During the last year of my service, I had seen my wife for a total of ten weeks, with forty-two weeks of separation. Furthermore, my baby daughter Donna was seventeen days old before I was informed of her birth and three months old before I saw her. I made the decision that I either stayed in the Army at the expense of my marriage and relationship with my wife and daughter or moved on to new pastures.

I started work at a plastics company working a sixty-five-hour week, picking up at the end of the week, fifty-four pounds. Things had to change. I transferred to nights as a material handler; after two years we were put on short time, I was working a split shift from 4 pm to midnight. Unbeknown to me the Managing Director had witnessed the way I was working and offered me a job as a trainee setter. This developed and I left the plastics company some eight years later as a qualified Plastics Technician and Senior Foreman.

While I was working in the plastics industry my wife gave birth to our second daughter, Rebecca on the 14th of September 1981, weighing in at 7 pounds eight ounces. Thinking I had done my bit for the world population we were surprised to find Julie pregnant a third time some six years after Rebecca had been born. Danielle was born on November 22nd 1988 weighing in at 6 pounds seven ounces. I spent a total of twenty-six years in the plastics trade, covering injection moulding, fabrication, extrusion moulding and the recovery of failing companies. I managed to develop several managerial skills and due to extensive experience working in various manufacturing companies, I knew they were transportable to other industries.

Determined to alter my lifestyle after Danielle had been born in 1988 having had my fill of boardroom backstabbing, I decided to look at doing something for myself. I pondered on this for a long period and decided to take casual work temping under an agency for six months; during this time, I had been offered three full-time jobs driving forklift trucks, however, working for someone else was not on my agenda. I had spent years working for others, doing 60/70/80 hours a week, being on call all hours to the detriment of family life and missing out on bringing up my children. I had a helping hand in changing my direction; after six months, Julie and I went on holiday with Danie to Spain and on our return, the economic crash hit. In two weeks, I had gone from picking from several jobs to finding I couldn't get any, things were going to have to change.

Eventually, I decided to start a business as a gardener; the overheads and initial outlay for equipment were quite low and it would not drain my bank account. Having done this for three years and established a small but successful business, I saw an opportunity to branch out into garden fencing. A few years on and thinking about my future, I won one of the largest lottery pay-outs on record.

2

Flexing my wealth

When it happens, let's just say it's a shock, it's hard to believe that life as you know it is going to change beyond all recognition. You would think that you would want to tell the world, and go out partying every night, it's not like that although I could understand anyone who did win wanting to follow that route. Julie my wife and I sat in our living room in complete shock, my youngest daughter, Danielle and future son-in-law, Jake, were buzzing and jumping around in sheer delight. We did nothing for two days apart from telling Danie and Jake to keep the knowledge to themselves until we had decided how we would move forward. That's like telling a politician to tell the truth. We did not know if we needed to contact a solicitor and seek advice or contact Lotto and see if they would advise us. We decided to contact Lotto and see where it would lead us.

I rang the number on the back of our winning lotto ticket and informed them I thought I had a winning ticket with all five numbers and both bonus numbers. I was asked to explain where I purchased the ticket and my name and address. The next step was to read to them the long number at the bottom of the ticket below the bar code so that they could authenticate my claim. I read out the numbers as requested, and then read out the winning numbers. To my surprise, I was told that they would confirm my ticket was authentic on inspection and it looked like I had secured a substantial win. I asked what I should do now and was told to sign the ticket with my name and address to secure the ticket as mine.

I asked how much the win was and felt disappointed and surprised that they said they would contact me directly to discuss my claim further. I informed them of my contact details and hung up the phone. Feeling disappointed and frustrated, we sat together thinking that maybe we had got it all wrong or something was not correct with our ticket. Maybe it was a freak week and thousands of people had won and the pay-out would be very minimal. Within a couple of hours, we had a phone call from Lotto HQ informing us that they would like to call at our house the following day or we could travel in a car they would send for us to Lotto headquarter in London to claim our winning. We asked that they send a representative to our home to discuss it with us.

That night neither Julie nor I slept, both feeling drained and excited at the same time, panicking that something would go very wrong. Midday on the Tuesday a posh car pulled up and two gentlemen in suits got out and walked up the path and knocked on our door. They introduced themselves and showed us some form of identification, they asked us to check with Lotto HQ to confirm their identity. We were also asked to confirm our identity and show them the winning ticket. They produced some small, hand-held machine to authenticate it was a genuine ticket. We were then congratulated and informed that we had won £117,998,147.47, the fourth largest win in lotto history to date.

We spent several hours in the company of these gentlemen discussing possible investments, security, and future plans. By the time they left, our heads were buzzing with information and concern that we were going to be swamped with forthcoming events. We asked that our privacy be maintained and our new friends informed us that with such a large win it would eventually leak out into the general population. Julie and I both sat down and started to consider what direction we wanted to take. We decided that we would need to see an accountant and solicitor about some of our immediate plans, such as giving our three daughters one million pounds each. I had long dreamt about such a win and like most people felt I knew what I would do, however when you are in that position your perspective most likely changes.

We started ringing around the next day trying to find a solicitor and accountant that we felt comfortable with and when you mention millions of pounds, it's surprising how many claimed to know best. We finally settled on one of each profession and arranged to have them visit us at home to discuss our plans. Can you imagine, an accountant or solicitor coming to your home to discuss if you were in some sort of trouble or needed some basic advice on your annual tax return? Our gut feeling turned out to be good, we felt comfortable in their presence and the advice they provided appeared to be sound. It was a further forty-eight hours before the money hit our account.

With the help and assistance of our solicitor and accountant, we transferred one million pounds into each of our daughter's accounts Donna, Rebecca and Danielle. We called a family meeting to explain what we had done for the girls and told them, what they did with it was up to them. We currently have nine grandchildren however, we stated that it was up to each of the girls what they gave to the grandkids. Our next task was to start looking for a new home. I wanted a large house with lots of land and Julie wanted to stay in our current house. I knew that it would take some convincing to get her to move, but I had a plan of my own to help change her mind. It took quite a few phone calls to get estate agents to accept we were genuine customers and get their thumbs out of their asses and start looking for us.

I had speculated that I wanted at least eight bedrooms, four reception rooms and all the normal rooms to boot. I also informed them I wanted lots of land. I was looking at trying to get an income from tenant farmers as well as developing my own projects. While the estate agents were attempting to look, we took the entire family on an all-paid holiday to Mauritius. We booked the top floor of a five-star hotel for two weeks and had a wonderful time. We were a party of seventeen and although we had some toddlers with us, we soon settled into a routine.

On our return to the UK, we all went our separate ways home. On our arrival, we were met at the door by several newspaper reporters and two sacks full of mail. We were told this may happen and politely walked past the journalists and sorted out the mail. All but three letters were of any importance, the remainder is still at the old house and I have to admit, we did not read any of them. I had quite a negative view of charities in general and if I were to support one myself, I would set my own up and not pay some fat cat to run it.

One of the three looking like a proper letter came from one of the estate agents informing us that they had a property in Kent meeting our requirements, with 2,000 acres of land and with the option from adjoining farmers for a possible further 750 acres. I telephoned the agent and arranged to view the property the following day. We had been advised to change our phone numbers by the Lotto team and within hours of our return, we understood why. We had car salespeople offering us new top-of-the-range cars on free trial periods for months; telephone companies asking us to swap to their network system with similar offers. Television personnel asked us to have an open format discussion on live television to inform people of our transformation from poverty to riches, it became quite sickening very quickly.

The following day, I went to Kent on my own to view the property. The house was empty as the owner had moved abroad for health reasons and the property was up for 27 million. I looked around and made a quick estimate that it would need some money spending on it to bring it up to an acceptable standard. It had nine bedrooms but only six had ensuites. On the ground floor were a large kitchen, two sitting rooms a study, a library, and several other rooms. I noticed a door that the estate agent had not mentioned and found it led down to a cellar with an additional four, nice size rooms. The heating system was old and would need replacing but, I was pleased to see an open fireplace in one of the sitting rooms as I loved having an open fire in the first house we bought when we came out of the Army. Nothing is better than an open fire on a cold miserable day.

On the outside, the roof had recently been replaced and the windows on the front of the property were new. The windows at the rear and side of the house needed to be replaced. The decoration was dated and I knew that Julie would want to alter it all around so was not concerned as far as that went. I asked about the tenant farmers and was told that the grounds were broken down into eleven farms of various sizes. Contacts were available but would need updating. I informed the agent that I would like to meet with each farmer and assess the farm and its buildings. It was quite clear that I would not be able to complete this task in a short time and so returned to the Midlands.

Two days later I received a call stating that arrangements had been made with all the tenants for the next two days, to view the properties and copies of the tenants' agreement were available for my inspection. I booked into a hotel for three nights in Kent and the estate agent met me the following day at 9 am. We visited all the eleven farms in the two days and I spent the following day going through the tenant agreements. Before I left, I organised through the estate agent to have aerial photographs taken of each farm and also the farm I had been told about that may also be up for sale. I also asked the estate agent to obtain an overall ordinance survey map to be broken down into each farm and connecting farms.

I returned to the Midlands once again and arranged to see the solicitor to go through the contracts with the tenant farmers. The solicitor informed me that by and large they appeared to cover most eventualities and would only need a little tweaking. I asked him to proceed with the work as quickly as possible should my offer be accepted. I had a couple of builders look at the photos I had taken to try to give me a rough estimate of the costs involved in the various repairs and alterations of what I had found during my visits to the farms and asked for guidance and estimate for repairs from what they could see from each property and the main house. Once I had calculated my figures and found out that the property was on the market because the owner needed to pay a hefty tax bill, I was ready to make my offer. Nothing gained nothing ventured. I offered £20,000,000 for the lot, subject to my solicitor making sure that there were no Covenants or hidden surprises. My offer was accepted very quickly leaving me concerned that I was missing something that would bite me at a later date.

The solicitors turned out to be very good and went

through everything with a fine-tooth comb. Six weeks later I was the proud owner of a 2,000 acres estate. All the new contracts were signed by the tenant farmers and the land re-distribution changes that I had been looking for were complete. While going around the farms, I had been looking for poor ground or low productive ground. I had managed to find two plots spread over four of the farms. For a reduction in rent at an acre rate and assurances from me that the rent would not rise for a year, all the farm tenants signed up. I now had 32 acres in one site and a mile away a further six acres. I had two main roads going through the farms and a small village on the left-hand side of the far extremities. I had engaged a small team of builders to oversee the restoration of the house, I had also instructed the foremen to apply for planning permission to build a five-car garage with office space above. The basics of my plans were starting to come together. I also arranged for decorators to start stripping the walls of the house to make sure that the plaster was not going to fall off. To my surprise, the inside of the house was in excellent condition so I cancelled the decorators and informed them that I would require their services in the near future. I had asked Ben the builder to work on the modifications, change the windows at the side and rear, make sure that each room had its own ensuite, and several other tasks that would keep him busy for a few weeks or months.

I asked Julie if she would come down to the new house the following day and help advise on wallpaper and fittings and fixtures. We arrived at ten am and met two people, one was a chap that had stripped the house of the old clutter and he had brought books and a Pantone colour book for Julie to choose what she felt was the right paper and paint. The next was a lady who talked about the design of wardrobes, beds, settees and soft furnishings and finally, a plumber who was looking at radiators, taps, toilets etc.

Ben had altered all the rooms around and as I had requested each room had its own ensuite, he had had no option other than to use one of the smaller rooms and transform it into ensuites for two of the bedrooms. This had reduced the house into an eight-bedroom house. Six weeks later and the house was complete, and I must say it looked superb. Each person we had called on had done their trade proud. Julie had spent hours at the new house and I knew she loved it. I couldn't see her refusing to move in, and that evening she said,

"So, when do we move down to the new house?"

We arranged a removal team the next day to start moving our stuff from the old house to the new one. They could not fit us in for a week and that gave us a little time to say goodbye to our old life. From this point on I was on a mission to build an empire that my children and grandchildren would be able to expand further for many years to come. Again, using the experience of the estate agent manager, I engaged the service of an architect to draw up plans on the thirty-two-acre site for the building of 1000 houses with as detailed guidance and as much detail as I could offer; and on the six-acre site to build fifty industrial units of various sizes. During the next week, I had numerous telephone calls from the architect discussing various options regarding play-parks, styles of houses, and the texture of brick; the list went on and on.

One of the issues the Architect could not quite grasp was I had given him a brief to utilise the pavements to avoid future road works and during poor freezing weather, stop the pavements from freezing. The final requirement for our home was to increase the security. The main entrance was covered by two electric gates, and I had decided to support these with CCTV with a monitor just inside the front door. I had a further six cameras installed around the external walls of the house and two cameras inside my office. The two hidden cameras in my office were wide lenses that could capture an all-round view and these also recorded audio. All the cameras were taken to a central point in the basement apart from the two for the main gate.

I had an idea to develop a system for roads that would almost eliminate further road works and make access to piping and services much easier than our current system. I contacted several fabrication and foam manufacturers and discussed what I had in mind. It took several weeks but, in the end, I had firm plans and designs that would further my plan. I had the prototype moulds made and asked a company run by Billy Nichols to do the trials, once these were completed, I had the smaller system that would go across the roads installed running down the side of the drive at home, this would allow planners etc to physically see how the system worked and its durability, and it gave us the opportunity to see how it performed while all the testing was being undertaken. From the samples being submitted and finally approved, it took over a year and I had a system that I felt would revolutionise this part of the industry. If the new system had not worked, I could have reverted to the old and tested system on traditional pavements.

I took out the necessary protection and arranged the patents to safeguard my development and had a better set of moulds made in readiness for what I had in mind. Basically, the product was made from expending reinforced foam with flame-retardant chemicals incorporated. The larger system weighed in at fifty kilos for the base and a further fifty kilos for the top, it was three meters long and one and a half wide and seven hundred mils deep. Inside, it was in two sections, one was for rain run-off from the road, and the second was for the services. One side of the road would be for water, gas sewage etc and the other side for anything electrical. For any cross sections going from one side of the road to the other, a smaller section that I had used on the driveway at home was used, split into two halves separating the services and allowing the services to cross the main road unhindered. As electricity and gas emit an element of heat, this would also stop the pavements from freezing during bad weather. In addition, the system was installed flat with the road and this would stop the need for pavement drop downs and as it was reinforced, it could take the weight of our largest lorries fully-loaded.

I knew I had taken a gamble in producing this system and the cost had been expensive but, I was committed to improving our current system and having obtained the approval of the product, wanted to use it on the housing estate I was planning on developing. One of the concerns was about its security; I had made the hinged lid extra-heavy and it could only be lifted by using a Hiab or crane; this prevented children from trying to tamper with the cables or pipes and also the services were covered by an internal plate so were not visible from the road. Costs compared to the traditional pavement system were quite compatible however, taking into account that the roads would not need to be dug up every time work was needed on any of the services, it was a winner from the start although, a number of large companies were having objections to it from the start as they saw it would have a huge impact on what they traditionally did.

3

Lining up the people
and positioning my pieces

I knew that to succeed with my plans, I had to have the right people in the right places, from builders to the local Mayor, Planning Office, local politicians and local law enforcement. In the early stages of my plans, I made appointments with various people and had an arranged meeting with some old colleagues about hidden CCTV for the house, visible CCTV for the outside and covert cameras for my person and in my study with audible abilities.

My first appointment was with the Chief Constable at 11 am on Wednesday, February 14th. I was shown into a nice office and offered coffee and biscuits. The Chief Constable appeared very pleasantly open and welcoming. He shook my hand and introduced himself as Sir Robert Barnes. I outlined my plans with him and asked for his advice on the security of the housing estate. I explained I wanted to build on the 32 acre-site that I had selected and wanted his opinion regarding the legal aspect and his personal view. He was all for it knowing that a larger population would allow larger funding and prosperity for the area. I asked if he was prepared to lend me his support when it came to planning and he warmly shook my hand with a big smile on his face; one on board. My second appointment was with the local mayor, Harry Tooland. I only realised after meeting Harry that the position, he held was only for twelve months unless re-elected. Nevertheless, he appeared to throw his full nine stones behind the project and offered his complete support should he still be in office; two down.

My next appointment was with the local MP Justin Harper, I felt that he would be key to the success of my plans and it wasn't until much later that I realised how instrumental and helpful he had been. I had arranged to meet him at his office in the village town hall as he used one of the rooms to conduct his surgery twice a week. He was much younger than I had expected and quite abrupt when I entered his office. I explained my plans for the development of the 32-acre site and also added my plans for 50 industrial units on the six-acre site. He appeared to be sceptical and guarded in his response. I informed him that the local Mayor and Chief Constable were behind my quest and his approach suddenly changed a little. I think at first, he may have felt I was trying to con him or something and only when he realised, I had already spoken to a couple of the local officials he opened up by informing me that he would look at trying to get central government funding and that I should not have to look at funding such a high-value project on my own.

It was quite clear that the project I had proposed regarding the pavements had caught his attention. He invited me to London the following week to explain my proposals to a group of gentlemen who were not that keen on stating their names. I felt quite uncomfortable and after my PowerPoint presentation, I was introduced to each one in turn and the atmosphere changed. To this date, I still do not know much about these gentlemen sitting around the table, but they opened a number of doors that I didn't know existed, three down.

Then I had the hardest task, getting the plans finalised and summiting them to the planning department and local council. I did not know how expensive drawing up plans and submitting them to the planning office could be. I proposed that the 32-acre site be divided into four sections. Plans would be drawn up for one section containing some 250 houses and then the plan rotated to form the plans for the other three plots and where possible the houses should have the back gardens facing south so they caught the maximum amount of sun. Included in the plans were to be two small parks, eight shops, an entertainment club with a bar, snooker club, restaurant and room for venues. On the six-acre site, I had asked the planners to draw up 35 units some 1000 square feet and 10 units some 4000/5000 square feet and five units of 10,000 square feet. I had in my mind other ideas regarding a garage complex, but this would have to wait until another time. I had recorded all my meetings and kept the recording very safe, only I knew about them and that's the way I wanted to keep it. We all hear about corrupt officials, if this turned out to be true, I would not hesitate to approach the right people to see justice done. I wanted my dreams and plans to be clean and free from corrupt bureaucrats, however, I know that during a large operation such as this at some stage I would witness it in full force.

My plans were submitted to the planning office in April 2007 with the support of all the above-mentioned and a promise of assistance regarding funding, if all were approved. I had requested that when the plans had been drawn up, I wanted to come away from the traditional method of laying pipes, power cables and services in every direction and I had requested that all services were routed through the pavements. I had quite a few strange looks. Why? was the obvious question. I wanted to utilise the entire pavement in the following way: firstly, the area would be dug out and the floor and walls lined with moulds made from expending foam mouldings, a dividing section splitting it in half. The half nearest to the road would be used for the traditional water run-off from the road. The other half would be used, on one side of the road for, power, TV connections etc. On the other side of the road, it would be used for gas, sewage and water. The top covering of the path would be made from the same material and the weight could only be lifted by a Hiab-type vehicle to prevent tampering and be open from the road. Any crossing of the road would be done through smaller channels made in the same style as on the pavement. The advantage of this was, no further road works would be digging up the road often just after they had been laid. During cold spells the heat generated from the sewage and electrical cabling would in the main, prevent the paths from becoming frozen.

The estimated costs were staggering. Planning was costed at one million pounds, ground works, it was estimated that the main services to the site (pipes, electric and gas, water, sewage waste water) were costed at eight million and my request for the idea I had regarding the layout through the paths instead of across the roads, added another one million making ten million pounds potentially spent and not a house to show. Due to the newness of the idea and the complexity of getting positioning correct, the basics of the road would have to be in place before any of the houses were built. These costings did not include the industrial park as that came into stage two of the housing park.

I discussed with the Chief Constable about security for the housing estate. I wanted to put a cost of £260 per annum on each house to have CCTV at every entrance to the estate, for security to walk around the estate at night, £260 per year for the smaller industrial units and £390/£520 per year for the larger ones. For the smaller shops, it would work out at £416 and for the larger units, restaurant and clubhouse, snooker club and venue room £780 per annum. The industrial estate would be surrounded on all sides and secured with palisade fencing eight feet high with individual digital entry to enter and leave the site, again the site would be visited twice per night by security. The security office would be sited in a central area adjacent to the restaurant and clubhouse. The idea is that the security is self-funding and non-profit making. It would be part of the contract when purchasing the property or renting, this would be passed on to any subsequent buyers and rentals.

The Chief Constable had an element of concern that it would be difficult to enforce and promised to look into the matter and come back to me within two weeks. In the meantime, I approached my solicitor and asked him to draft a contract, to show the Chief Constable what I was looking at. On top of having it as part of the purchase of the house, the buyer would have to agree that they paid a security fee monthly. Caravans and large vans were not permitted to be parked on drives or grass for more than forty-eight hours twice a year, and gardens were to be maintained to a reasonable standard, ie grass cut etc. If the owner became incapable of maintaining the garden, it was their responsibility to hire help. Having lived on a housing estate, I knew how it felt to have one neighbour lovingly keep their garden, while the people next door allowed theirs to become overgrown. Not only that, it certainly didn't help, if your neighbour failed to keep their garden good when you're trying to sell your house. I knew this would make a few people's eyebrows go up but, I wanted to create a pleasant environment for people to live in and where they felt safe and secure. I hoped in time that the residents would form their own committee that would become self-governing.

In two separate conversations with Harry Tooland and Justin Harper, they highlighted what they considered to be a potential problem. They were both concerned that although a small school was established in the village, it would not be able to accommodate thousands of new students, also that the nearest hospital was eleven miles away. Justin had told me that he would look at government funding for his concerns regarding the school and he felt confident that the other issue was addressed within the plan. Although we were some time away from starting the plan, and even further away from its conclusion, I felt this may scuttle the whole development. Justin came back to me surprisingly early two days later stating, that should the project be accepted by the local authorities, funding would be granted to extend the local hospital and develop the existing school into an academy as well as Junior and Infants schools being expanded. Justin told me that he would be present when the plans were submitted to the town hall and would highlight these issues and explain the financial advantages of expanding the village/town.

The planning proposal had been submitted and a date for the hearing was set for three weeks away. I think I was on tenterhooks for the whole three weeks March the 24th 2008 was the date of the council committee's sitting, fourteen months since I had won the lottery and a lot of my plans were hanging on the decision within the next couple of hours. I had to be there in person and present the proposal in detail. I noticed some friendly faces on the committee and started my proposal. Once I had completed my presentation, almost straight away the subject of schooling and emergency services came up. Justin jumped in stating that he had been assured by his colleagues that should the committee approve this application in principle, funding would be made available for the developments of the schools and expansion of the local hospital. The only other objection came from a local councillor who had concerns about the noise and disruption this would have on the small village. Harry Tooland came to my rescue by saying that we could not sit still while the rest of the world evolved and needed to move with the times.

At the end of all the talking, I was asked to leave the room while they had a further discussion. Twelve people were deciding the fate of my proposal and holding my future dreams in their hands. I went through who was at the meeting and out of the twelve, I felt that I had half the votes in my favour and for the other six, I had not got a clue. I knew that to get it passed, I had to have a two-thirds majority. Forty-five minutes later, I was called back in to be told that in principle the application was granted, subject to what Justin had claimed to be granted. I thanked the committee and walked out feeling fantastic. Finally, my dream was starting to come true and a great weight had been lifted from my shoulders.

I rang Justin and Harry that evening and thanked them for their help and support. I knew that they had both assisted in the meeting in turning it in my favour and had they not, it may have not been approved. Harry told me that I was welcome to his support and that someday I may be able to repay the favour. The way he said it gave me pause for thought and worried me a little but I didn't know why. On the drive home after the meeting, I reflected on the events of the past few hours and realised how lucky I had been to have achieved this result. Once I got home, I told Julie all about what had happened but did not mention the conversation I had with Harry.

4

Slow progress - The People

While I was working my butt off trying to develop my project, the camera system had been installed. I had asked my girls Donna, Rebecca and Danielle and their partners to relocate to Kent as I dearly wanted an all-family operation. (Let's face it, there's nothing more loyal than Daddy's little girl and I have three of them.) After we had moved into our new home, the next project Ben Sykes my foreman of the builders had on his books was to start on the five-car garage with offices above. Ben had secured planning permission and work was due to start in two weeks. I wanted to have a garage for each of Julie's and my car as well as storage space for the lawn mower and other gardening equipment. Above, the offices would serve as a boardroom, an office for my personal assistant and one for the purchase clerk and an office each for Ben and Jonathan.

Ben estimated two months with his team of five men. I told him that I was impressed with the work ethic that he and his lads had shown working on the house and offered him a job working directly for me along with his whole team. I briefly outlined my plans and asked how he felt about heading the operation. During discussions with Ben over the past few weeks, I knew Ben had extensive knowledge and a wealth of experience as he had headed up large operations for some of the big housing companies and this would be invaluable for my organisation in the near future.

An old pal of mine that I had been working with for a few years doing garden fencing, Dave, was struggling with the heavy demands of his job and I wanted him at my side and together with his wife, Alison, leading the personnel side of the business. I made a telephone call to Dave and asked him and Alison to come down to stay with us for the weekend. When they arrived, I showed Dave and Alison the progress we had made since we had last seen them. I explained what we were looking at and the future development programme and then made my offer to them both. My mate jumped at it, all we had to do was convince his better half Alison to accept the job on offer to her. I knew that it would be a big wrench to up sticks and move away from family and friends. She had worked for the same company for many years and needed a change but she was loyal to her current employer and company. I knew it would take some persuading and that is why I had asked them both to come down to the new house for the weekend to discuss my proposal; I wanted good friends at my side for the journey I was undertaking and a friend that you can trust and respect is worth a lot. I asked them both to consider my proposal and think it over during the following week. I did not want to leave it any longer as things were starting to move fast and if they did not accept my offer, I would need to find satisfactory replacements.

I kept my relationship going with my new pals, local Mayor Harry Tooland, Chief Constable Sir Robert Barnes, local MP Justin Harper and Chief Planning Officer, Malcolm Johnson and decided to spend some time getting to know them better. I invited the Chief Constable and his good lady, Kelly, down to the new house the following weekend, the day after Dave and Alison had been down. Robert and I hit it off from the start. He had been knighted by Her Majesty Queen Elizabeth II in 2006 for services to the crown; he had been awarded bravery medals five times and served in the police force since the age of seventeen.

He was now pushing 53 years of age and fighting like cat and dog to remain a police officer. They expected him to retire at 55 but he claimed that was age discrimination. He was a man who loved his work; he told me that's what got him out of bed in the morning and kept him active and sane. Due to his senior position, he couldn't be put behind a desk or used as front of office at the local nick. They had proposed a position working in an advisory capacity to the government on policing strategies and funding issues that may be available when he did retire. As he said to me, this was a lot of bull; six months down the line this position would become redundant and he'd find himself on the scrap heap.

Robert and I talked for hours; our lives were so different and yet we found ourselves on similar paths. I explained to him that prior to the lotto win, I was thinking about my future retirement and what I would need to do in only a few years. I was trying to give Robert some enthusiasm but he saw right through me, smiled and thanked me for trying. We had a laugh about my pathetic efforts.

By now we had engaged a housekeeper, Sandra, a cook, Martha, and a gardener, Billy. Martha had excelled herself with the meal she cooked. The first course was pumpkin soup followed by roast beef with all the trimmings and a toffee sponge with custard to finish us off and it did. I was eager to try out my new snooker table while the ladies settled down in the living room wishing they had worn elasticated clothes. Robert beat me three games to none and I suspected he was not a copper but a con man out to fleece me. It's a good job we weren't playing for money. While we were playing snooker, Sandra came in and handed me the phone. Dave was on the line to tell me that both he and Alison would love to accept the positions I had offered them. I told Dave I would cover all moving finances and asked him to come down as soon as possible. He said they could be with me within a fortnight and some of the packing would be completed by their daughters after they had moved down.

Robert and Kelly clearly enjoyed the evening and when it got to eleven o'clock, I called a taxi to take them home. The next morning Robert called at 10.30 to collect his car and said that he and Kelly had enjoyed one of the best nights in a very long time. He came in for coffee and left an hour later. We were nurturing a friendship that would last for years and we became the very best of friends.

A couple of nights later, Julie and I were out at what was now our local curry house when Harry Tooland and his wife Martha walked in. Some mix-up in booking had left them with no table and looking quite embarrassed, especially when Harry saw me witnessing what was going on. Harry was just about to leave when I invited him and Martha to come and join us. We had only arrived five minutes before so were still waiting to place a drinks order and looking through the menu. He appeared a little guarded and Martha was almost hostile. We talked about our children and a little of our history when Harry told us that they had made the decision not to have children. He had been a welder and fabricator in the docks for thirty years, and they offered him redundancy, he decided to accept it and they moved further north up into Kent. He had tried to get various jobs and almost fell into politics. After working in the town hall, he eventually applied for the position of Mayor and was fortunate enough to get it.

The evening went off ok, but there was an undercurrent that I could not fathom. I paid for all our meals and drinks and later at home when I was sitting and thinking about the evening, I decided that Harry and Martha were not very nice people. They were in the position they were in to get what they could out of it. I knew that he would be the one to watch and I half expected trouble in the future. I also knew that I would not be spending any further evenings with Harry and Martha unless in it was in a professional capacity.

A few days later, I had a phone call from Justin who was mainly based in London, inviting Julie and me down to his cottage retreat in St Ives in Cornwall. As a boy, I had spent some time on holiday in St Ives and was looking forward to revisiting. We made the arrangements and arrived late on a Friday afternoon, greeted by Sally, Justin's wife and his two children, Clair and Justin Junior. Having not met Sally before we were a little apprehensive but, she was so warm and welcoming, we felt comfortable from the off. She invited us in and showed us our room. She was a wonderful host and put us at our ease from the second the door opened. Clair was eleven years old and Justin Junior was nine. Sally told us all about how she and Justin met and how they had been married for fourteen years. She had been his secretary when they first met and love had blossomed. Prior to arriving both Julie and I were apprehensive about our visit, after all, Justin was a Member of Parliament, and we were sure we would feel out of place. We had been at the cottage for just under an hour when Justin arrived and apologised profusely for not being at home to welcome us. We explained that Sally had been a wonderful host and they should look at opening up a hotel, her welcome alone would guarantee they'd never have an empty room.

We spent two days at the cottage marvelling at some wonderful scenery and managing to find the house I stayed in as a boy. We could not go in but it was nice to have a look around and just to know it was still there. Justin's children were some of the best-behaved kids I have known, always well-mannered and both of them in bed by nine pm, when we settled down with a glass of wine and chatted about anything and everything. Justin was expected to be appointed to the cabinet in the near future and he was hoping to get the position of Housing Minister, having had a lot of involvement with development programmes over the past five years. It then became a little clearer why he had shown such interest and knowledge in my plans from the off. We did not retire until gone 3 am and our concern was that Sally would have two youngsters jumping all over her at an ungodly time in the morning. Our concerns were unwarranted, we got up at around 9 am only to find Sally already cooking breakfast and the two little ones dressed and playing on their consoles. We knew that Justin had work back in London on Monday morning so after a fabulous lunch we made our excuses and headed back home on Sunday afternoon. We could not thank Justin and Sally and the kids enough for being such warm and wonderful hosts.

We returned the offer to come and stay at our house the following month and they both jumped at the invitation. Once again, we felt we were nurturing a warm and friendly new relationship. Our only concern was that Justin and Sally were in their early forties, whereas we were in our early to mid-fifties, we just hoped that they would see past this and see us for the people we were.

On the way back home with Julie driving, I was free to make some calls, the first was to Dave and Alison to see if they were ok with what we had discussed and apologising for not being able to talk much when Dave rang me. I had offered Dave and Alison the opportunity to stay with us until he managed to find suitable accommodation, but he said that they had already found their own house in the local village. On our return home as we pulled up, Ben Sykes my builder was waiting at the house, he had come to work on a Sunday (this, in my opinion, showed his work ethic) to tidy off a couple of things. Ben and I went into the study and Martha brought in some coffee. Once we were settled, I asked Ben what was troubling him. He explained that the offer I had made had been playing on his mind. His concerns were who would do the recruitment, purchasing of goods and security of the site? Both Ben and I knew that the building work was due to start big time, and this was one of his concerns as to what he and his team would be doing after the site had been completed. I told Ben that the buildings on the farms needed work conducting on them. Two needed new roofs, and a barn needed to be rebuilt; two of the houses needed new windows and several walls needed re-pointing. In addition, some of the outbuildings needed attention, possibly rebuilding. As for the concerns, my view was that as far as recruitment went, he was the main employer; if he needed assistance, I would lend him the help of Alison to conduct interviews and reduce numbers down to two or three candidates. All paperwork would be passed to Alison for security and background checks. Alison would write letters of offer and draw up contracts of employment. Regarding the purchase of goods, again one of the offices being built above the garage would be used as a purchasing office and what Ben would need to do, is simply pass on the requirements to Alison who would be responsible for providing a purchasing clerk. This was a concern that I felt he did not need to worry about, and I said that it would be a gradual build-up of staff. While the ground works were being done it would give a window of a few months to recruit.

I explained that Alison and Dave would be starting on

Monday and asked Ben to come to the house so I could introduce him to them both. Security would be done in two ways; first contractors would secure the outer perimeter and one man would be hired to maintain security overnight, any additional security would be looked at as and when and I would ask Dave to help oversee this issue. Ben and I discussed several other minor points and by the end of our conversation, I think Ben was more than happy with what we had discussed and was confident and relieved he would have the help he knew he would need to fulfil his role. Ben and I talked through until late that evening and I asked him about his family. Ben had been married to Jill for twenty-two years and they had two children, Brian the eldest aged twenty-one- and twenty-year-old Tom. I did not realise that both worked with Ben as part of his team. One of Ben's other employees was William who had worked for Ben since leaving school while Tony had only just joined him a few months earlier.

Ben left at almost midnight, and I was confident his concerns were set aside. My final comment was that he would need to construct the garage and office complex as quickly as possible in order to give us a central operations point. I also informed Ben that I had other projects in mind that would hopefully ensure his employment until retirement.

That night I did not sleep well, I don't know why but I was up early the next morning only to find Martha and Sandra sitting in the kitchen drinking tea. Both jumped when I walked in and I had to smile to myself. I told them to sit and finish their drinks and I joined them. Martha our cook was responsible for the day-to-day ordering of supplies and doing the meals under the direction of Julie. Martha had worked for years in a care home only a couple of miles away and unfortunately, it had closed down six months ago. Martha had been looking for any kind of work but being past fifty all doors appeared to be shut. When Julie interviewed her, she said she knew within five minutes that Martha was the correct choice. Martha was a widow and had been for several years, she had a son Josh who lived in Australia that she had not seen for two years. She talked to him on a fairly regular basis and missed him terribly. She could not drive a car and cycled to and from work just over a mile away. Martha's deceased husband had left her and Josh in a financial pickle, it had taken Martha six years to get out of the financial restraints and now she lived in rented accommodation above a shop in the village. On the other hand, Sandra our housekeeper was a live wire, she was as loud and chirpy as anyone could be. She had an infectious personality that everyone warmed to. Everyone felt comfortable in her company, and she was the housekeeper from heaven and was responsible for the housekeeping internally. Julie was a good cook, but Martha took it to another level. Whenever anyone came to the house, if Martha was on duty they were fed with cakes, and homemade biscuits and if they were on a second visit to the house, Martha would have their favourite cake or biscuits on hand. If we were entertaining family or friends, often Martha would cook a meal that would outshine any Michelin-starred restaurant. Sandra was thirty-two and liked to bat for the other side. She did not hide her sexual preference, and no one gave it a second thought. She was a lovely woman and I trusted both Martha and Sandra implicitly. Sandra had been out of work for two years prior to coming to us and had not really tried to get a job. Martha's passion was cooking and the role she had found with us fulfilled all her wishes. I think she thought, and we thought it was a job for life; both Martha and Sandra felt at home.

The last person on my immediate team would be William our gardener; he was twenty-four with a few little learning difficulties. Once William understood what was required, he would work until told to stop. This was more than a job to William, it was his independence, security, his whole world. He had a good brain although a little faulty wiring. His duties involved cutting the grass of which we had a lot, our lawn covered seven acres and William's pride and joy was the sit-on lawnmower. He had a good knowledge of plants and shrubs passed on by his mum and he used this to maintain the shrubs around the outside of the house. He polished the lawnmower every time it was used and ensured it was stored dry and safe once he was finished with it. He did not talk much to people and if he went missing at any time, I knew he would be sitting in the kitchen with Sandra or Martha. He lived six miles away and his mum, Helen who attended his interview dropped him off every day and picked him up in the evening. Helen was eternally grateful that we had employed William as getting a job with his issues in such a small village would have been very difficult. I told Helen after a couple of weeks that we were the lucky ones to find William.

As work was quiet at the moment, I asked Dave to give William a hand at developing the walled garden. My plan for Dave would come into effect when the building project started, I wanted to use Dave as a trouble-shooter wherever a problem arose. Dave had a good experience over a wide area, and I knew I would be able to drop him into almost any part that was failing or not moving quickly enough. The area covered around half an acre and was well overgrown, I told William that I would like him to make the house self-sufficient during the summer months with the produce he could grow. William did not like being idle.

Two weeks later Alison had taken to her role like a duck to water and had temporarily set up office in one of the rooms not used for anything next to my study. Dave was floundering a little as I had not defined his role and was using him as my ears and eyes. I was convinced that Dave's role would be more defined as time went by and while we both had some spare time available it gave us the opportunity to use the snooker table. Dave also used a small digger to help clear the walled garden with Ben.

5

Holiday time

I had promised Julie that we would have more holidays now we were getting older. Neither of us wanted to get to the stage where we became too old or incapable of enjoying a holiday. We had also asked my brother and his wife Jean, and Barry if they like would to join us. With all the turmoil following the win of the lottery, it had been shelved while I got the basics of my plans into position. I could not do a great deal while awaiting the start of the ground works and Ben and Alison were very busy ordering huge stocks of materials in readiness for starting the houses, so it was time to look at going away.

During my absence, I asked my future son-in-law Jonathan to be a point of contact for anyone who needed assistance or information. None of the kids had moved down at this stage although Jonathan had travelled down on a number of occasions, and I had used him for support and guidance. We had booked a cruise with an Italian company called M.S.C. The ship was called Devina and it would take thousands of passengers. We booked the holiday to depart in May 2008 for two weeks returning on a Saturday, this would hopefully give me the opportunity to be brought up to speed on current events through Jonathan, prior to meeting with everyone arranged on the Monday.

We had to fly from London to Miami to meet up with the ship. On the ship, we had cabins next to each other and a large balcony so we could sunbathe in private if we wanted to. It was our first cruise and we had been looking forward to having some sun and warmth. The ship was sixteen decks high and it was very easy to get lost when trying to get from one place to the other. We could not believe what was on board, bowling alleys, casinos, massive theatres that had fantastic shows, shops of all types, restaurants on every level ranging from A la carte to what Julie and Jean called the cattle run, this is where I felt most at home, it must have been being in part of the forces for so long it was a bit like a free for all.

We departed from Miami at 7 pm and spent the first two days at sea. We went to one of the shows every night and found the quality of entertainment outstanding. I found it incredible how such a large vessel could manoeuvre in and out of port with such ease; if you were not watching it leave the port you would not know you were moving. The ship was well over one hundred metres long and we had paid for what is called a 'drinks package', which meant that all drinks soft and alcoholic were included. Our first stop was at Philipsburg (St Maarten) we were allowed off the ship for the best part of the day and had to return by six pm. We had a good walk around and did some shopping. The shops were a little disappointing, I was not sure what to expect but I felt that we were cattle to the slaughter as is the case in many tourist towns.

On day five of the holiday, we docked at San Juan (Puerto Rico) at eight am and again spent the day ashore shopping and seeing the sights. We managed to find a nice little beach and enjoyed a swim in the sea; you could swim on the ship 24/7 if you wanted to but being in the sea, I felt is always nicer when the water is nice and warm. Day six was at sea all day and Barry and I booked the mini golf for a few hours. I managed to get Barry drunk and considering he did not drink much it was great to see him relax and get into the game. He cheated like hell but then so did I, so we called it a draw.

Then on day seven, we docked in the Bahamas. All I can say is what a place, we were on our way back to the ship when we were stopped by a street trader trying to sell me a wristwatch. He started off at 100 euros and could see we were not biting. Julie was firm and told him we were not interested but he would not give up. I must say I really did like the watch, but when Julie told him again to go, he became rude. We started to walk off when Barry gave him ten Euros for the watch and passed it to me. The girls were not happy; I loved the watch; it was gold in colour and one of those that automatically wound itself up as long as you wore it for a short time each day.

On day eight we returned to Miami in the States but never left the ship as we were only there a short while to replenish stocks. We then started to almost reverse our voyage but not visiting the same places and having another day at sea we stopped at Jamaica. While we were there, we decided to hire one of the local Taxis for the day rather than sticking with the crowd or booking some sort of trip through the ship's entertainment package and headed out on our own. The Taxi driver's name was Arrold; he was a really nice guy and took us around a big chunk of the island. We spent several hours with Arrold and he had plenty to show us. We definitely made the right decision to go in our own taxi and not follow everyone else. He told us about how he lived and some of the local culture, what sort of standard of living people were expected to have on as little as two US dollars a day.

As we travelled around, suddenly someone would jump out from the side of the road and start somersaulting along the road in front of the car. Arrold told us that this was how some of the locals made their living by performing acrobatics for a few dollars reward from the tourists. Arrold got us back to the ship with a good half hour to spare and we could not thank him enough for what he had done. The cost was very fair and value for money and we made sure Arrold got a good tip.

Security on the ship was impressive; each time we left or returned our bags were scanned. Each passenger was given a photo identification card to match the image on the computer monitor in the ship's register as you went through the door. The delay in getting on and off the ship was quite minimal but it gave a feeling that security was good and tight and we were in safe hands. One of the things that I had constantly on my mind when not on board was getting back to the ship on time. If you missed its departure, it was your responsibility to arrange transport or flight to meet the ship at its next docking location. The only thing I found a little disappointing was that we had been told we needed to pack suits, smart casual wear etc for more formal nights. I had gone out and bought an evening suit and casual suit on this guidance. The first time we went to a formal evening dinner, people were in casual clothes. I could have saved myself a small fortune and I did not particularly like dressing up formally.

Day eleven was at the Cayman Islands and we went to HELL, literally, the place was called HELL. It consisted of a small souvenir shop and a post office where you could send a letter home postmarked, I have been to Hell. Day twelve was spent in Mexico and we decided to get a taxi and ask the driver to take us around for the day. He took us to a tequila farm where we were offered tequila at over-inflated prices, we had already priced it up in the shops and they were asking three times that. We found the taxi drive disappointing and wished we had taken a different choice.

On our last visit of the cruise, we were back in the Bahamas for the second time for a few hours and finally, we were back in Miami on day fourteen ready for our flights home. The flight was long and tiresome, and by the time we got home, we were only fit to go to bed. The next morning after a good night's sleep Julie claimed she was ready for another holiday and started looking almost straight away. I had really enjoyed the holiday and it felt good to spend time with Barry and Jean but felt it was time to get back to work. We knew we would look forward to booking another holiday with them again as this had been the first time we had gone with another couple.

I was ready to return to work two days later as things were very busy. I had left instructions with various people and wanted to talk to Jonathan to bring me up to date prior to talking to everyone else. During the holiday I had decided that I would not work anymore on Sundays as I would make Sunday a family day. I was still managing a sixty-hour week but at least I was home every night and could knock the odd day off if I chose to, not that I ever did. The Lottery win changed all that. During my briefing with Jonathan and several other members of the team, I received a call from the estate agent that showed me our home. He told me that the farm we had discussed some eighteen months ago had finally come up for sale. He had been approached by the seller and asked to approach me as he had heard that I had been good and looked after my tenants. The farm involved seven hundred and sixty acres broken down into two tenant farms each with two hundred and fifty acres and one area where the owner himself lived of 260 acres. Each farm had a four-bedroomed house, two barns and a number of small outbuildings. The asking price was £3,500,000 and it came with a combine harvester, two tractors and several trailers.

I informed the estate agent that I was interested and arranged to go and see each of the farms ending up at the third farm which was the owner of all three. I asked Ben to accompany me so that he could make an assessment of each building for us to make a tally at the end. Both of the first two farms were in excellent condition but both houses required attention. One had a leaking roof and the other needed the roof replaced. Electrics all needed to be re-wired and the central heating systems replaced. All four barns were in good order and the farms were clean and tidy. The two farmers and the owner were welcoming and introduced us to their wives and families. On the main farm, the house was in excellent condition but one of the outbuildings was falling down and the other one was in good shape. He had three barns; one was used for the storage of the farm machinery.

The gentleman that was selling was a Mr Miles. He was a short man with a round, red face and spoke with a real southern accent. Being originally from the south, I understood him quite well. If I had just come from the Midlands and never spoken to a deep southern person, I would have found it hard to understand him. He told me that the tenants both had tenancy agreements that had lapsed, and the farms were now on a monthly agreement with a three-month notice period from either party. I asked several questions about the rents the equipment, the state of the houses, livestock and vehicles. Mr Miles answered all my questions and I found him to be a frank and honest person. I told him that I would consider his proposal and get back to him within a week.

As we were leaving, I asked the estate agent what he felt

the farms were worth on the open market. He told me that if it went onto the open market, he would want two per cent as a fee, and he would likely only get around 3 million. On my return home I contacted my solicitor and asked him to draw up the paperwork for the acquisition, Then I called Jonathan and asked him to find out what he could about Mr Miles. I then spoke to Alison to search Companies House, land registry, and a contact we had made at the bank to see if we could obtain any financial understanding of how the farms and tenancies were faring.

The following day the first to come back to me was Alison. She told me that the land had one public right of way running on the edge of the far corner of the first farm we had visited. The finances of the farms were fair but not good. All three farms belonged to Mr Miles and had been in his family for almost two hundred years. The following day the Solicitor rang to say he had drawn up a contract for the sale of Mr Miles's farm and wanted to know what price to put on it. I told him I would get back to him as soon as possible. I telephoned the estate agent and told him my offer was 2.5 million pounds for all we discussed including the farm machinery and that I would draw up the paperwork and be ready to transfer the money as soon as the legal documents were signed. The estate agent came back to me within the hour stating Mr Miles would not accept less than 2.55 million and he would be ready to sell within two weeks. I agreed the price, called the solicitor and asked him to send Mr Miles the contract. At no time had the reasons for the sale been discussed and it was only an afterthought that I felt it needed an explanation. I telephoned the estate agent and posed the question. He told me that Mr Miles had lost the enthusiasm for farming and that he had no sons to carry it on. He did have a daughter who showed no interest in farming and had moved to

London to follow her career in fashion.

True to Mr Miles's word he was ready to sell within two weeks. As the farms were Agricultural and Mr Miles had agreed with me and the other two tenants that we would allow Mr Miles's farm to be split between them both and they would reap the harvest when ready. Eighteen days after seeing the farms the contracts were signed and our estate had grown by a further seven hundred and sixty acres. I spoke to Ben about a timing scale for completing the work required and agreed with him that he may need a couple more members for his team. Alison had got herself established and was soon involved in the recruitment. I asked Ben how things were going and if he was finding things helpful with Alison taking the pain of the paperwork off his shoulders. He told me that when I first approached him about this paperwork, he said it was one of his biggest headaches. He had deliberately moved away from working for a large company as he was being run ragged and had set up his own company some twenty years ago because of the amount of paperwork involved. He was never given any support and expected to do paperwork at home in his own time. On top of this, he had to oversee the purchase of materials and monitor the site all at the same time. He stated that had I not agreed or offered to employ a purchasing clerk and someone to do a lot of the paperwork, he would never have accepted the position. He felt that now he could give the job his full attention and although he still had to do some paperwork it was manageable.

I felt at ease in Ben's company and had a great deal of respect not only for his approach to work but his skills and qualifications in multi-levels and trades. Both Ben's sons had followed in his footsteps and were both accomplished in carpentry, electrical installation, plastering and bricklaying. The other young lad that Ben employed, Ben had put him through college, and he was qualified in plumbing. This just left the youngster as we called him, at seventeen he was the lackey, fetching this taking that and making the tea etc. and from what I could see he was learning from some of the best. Ben's team were five and this was about to become seven, should the plans come to anything we would be needing a lot more staff in the near future.

I asked Ben what he would do about his own company. He said that with what we had agreed, he would fold up the company and put his sole effort into the projects that we discussed lay ahead. He also said that with the plans I had discussed he could not see a long-term future for a small company like his as it would get swallowed up by the large developments I was planning. He had been happy with the family business he had developed and knew that it would survive in some form or the other regardless of what I did but, what I had offered was a secure and very prosperous future and he felt he would have been a fool to turn it down.

6

We have a movement

By now we had been in our new home for just over eighteen months. In a short time we had sorted out quite a lot but, at the back of my mind was the expansion of the business. The plans I had were now approved by the local council and by the planning department and we had started work on the site. I decided to visit the planning office to check if there was any enthusiasm for any future developments. I was shown into a room and introduced to Malcolm Johnson. He looked to be in his thirties, a big chap with the appearance of a bodybuilder, not what you would expect from a pen pusher. I introduced myself and told him the reasons for my visit. He explained that my proposal for further development plans was acceptable, however, he had several issues with some of the more basic issues of the parks and the proximity of the clubhouse to some of the houses, but they had been ignored. I asked what distance he felt was appropriate and his response threw me. He stated that it was not for him to tell me how far away they should be but for me to submit the plans to an acceptable standard. It sounded like double talk, and I listened to his comments, wrote them down and thanked him for his time.

I went straight over to my architect's offices and explained what the planning officer's concerns were. George the head planner stated he had expected that and had deliberately drawn the plans like that to give them something to bitch about. He had a second set of drawings ready to go and advised me to submit them in two days. This being done, I left it two days as suggested before I made a second appointment with Malcolm in the planning office. Prior to leaving to go and see Malcolm I telephoned Justin and asked if he had any advice. He told me that if I felt I was being given the run around that I should mention that he was involved and that the Lord Mayor, Chief Constable and himself were all behind this project.

When I got to the planning office, Malcolm was not available, and I met with a gentleman somewhat older. He informed me that the plans were acceptable and stated that full planning permission would be granted immediately. I could not believe my ears. I think Justin may have helped swing the balance by something he said on the phone before I went to the planning office, anyway it had been passed on the 24th of August 2008 and we had been given the green light some eighteen months since we won the lotto and sixteen months since we submitted the planning application.

One of the first steps was to secure the site so children and foolish adults could not injure themselves on machinery or fell down holes. I asked Dave to organise a contract company to erect secure fencing all around stage one of the build. We then installed a porta cabin for the security guard. Ben then came into his own; at this stage, he did not need his team and left them under the supervision of his eldest son, Brian. Ben had already arranged the ground workers and they were awaiting his call and would be on site by the following Monday. All the ground works were conducted by a team of professionals, they knew what they were doing and were best left to get on with it.

Some major pipes and wiring would be installed and connected to the main sewer and water outlets. Although the main work would be down to the ground workers, the final connections would be down to the water, gas and electric companies. It was estimated to take three months to have the ground works completed on this first stage. In a few weeks, the contractor that installed the perimeter fencing would be back to install the same around stage two. When they had completed this they were to go to the industrial site and secure that. No security was planned for the industrial site as yet as it was only a fenced-off area with nothing to steal. However, Phillip the security guard was to flit between both sites at least two or three times during his shift.

One week early, the ground work was complete and passed off. I had asked my mate Dave to oversee the installation of the perimeter palisade fencing and electric gate to the industrial site. Dave had run his own company for many years doing fencing and he knew the job inside out. I had no one in a better position to ask and trusted to do a really good job so I asked Dave to oversee the contractors. On the first stage the following week, three and a half months into the project the first footings were being filled and the slabs followed shortly afterwards. During this period, Alison under Ben's guidance was conducting interviews with builders, electricians, carpenters, roofers, plumbers, and labourers. As soon as the ground workers completed one stage of the development, they moved to the second. At the end of stage two, they were to start on the industrial site; the ground workers could always swap back to Phase three and four once the rest had been completed. I wanted to see if I could encourage these skills sectors into the area and utilise some smaller companies to step up and enlarge their operation and possibly utilise some of the industrial units I wanted to build.

The first house was completed in March 2009. This was set up as a show home until the shops were completed. I asked my daughter's partner, Jonathan, to set up the show home and organise staff and the required paperwork for leaflets, sales contracts and a ton of other basic requirements too numerous to mention. Jonathan is a qualified Estate agent and also qualified to conduct Energy Performance Certificate, a vital legally required document to sell the new houses. These would all individually require an E.C.P. prior to selling to show that they are basically insulated correctly, airtight and that the thermal bridging was correct. Ben had now brought his team over and had increased his numbers to seventeen. We now had three brickies, three carpenters, two plasterers, two electricians, Ben and six semi-skilled labours.

At this stage, I knew that it would take years to complete all the plans I wanted and was impatient to keep pushing forward. Due to Ben and his team having to move over to the main development, my garage and office above were only half complete; I needed this to get finished as soon as possible because I wanted to use the offices as a centre of operations. I approached Ben and asked what he could do. After a few choice words from him, (I guess he was feeling the pressure) he agreed to send a brickie and a labourer over and rotate skills as required. The look on Ben's face told me my place and I quickly thanked him and walked away before he had a chance to change his mind.

One month later we were heading to Christmas and a three-week shutdown. During the months since planning had been approved, we had managed to erect sixty-seven houses that were in a state of partial completion, but the good news was that my garage was complete and the offices ready to move into. I tasked Alison and Dave to organise furnishings for the offices and set them up. We had snow on the ground, and I knew that no building work would start until the temperature had risen.

Eagar to get an update from all involved, I called a meeting in one of the new offices with Ben, Alison, and Jonathan. While doing the arrangements, I had a call saying one of the tenant farmers, Arthur, had been rushed into hospital following an accident on his farm and would be in hospital for another week. I guess it's times like these that you find out who your friends are. Two of Arthur's neighbours went over and looked after his live-stock and kept things ticking over. Fortunately, their farms were agricultural, so it was a quiet period for them and it was nice to know that the farmers had a good sense of solidarity to fall back on, should things such as this happen. Jonathan then showed us the literature he had organised for the showrooms and stated that he had already arranged for a lady called Sarah to work in the show home 10 am to 3 pm Wednesday, Thursday, Friday, Saturday and Sunday. She had worked in a showroom before and then moved into an estate agency and Jonathan felt she would be a good fit with her experience. I asked Alison to arrange for me to pay a visit when Arthur was up to it. Bob informed me that while this cold spell was on us little could be done as far as building was concerned, however, the ground work at the industrial site would be starting tomorrow and that over the Christmas period he had managed to recruit two more brickies, two plumbers, two decorators and another carpenter. I had taken on all of Ben's team as employees of my company, so Ben had arranged various jobs at some of the farms that needed work done inside. All the other chaps working on the project were contractors ie self-employed.

One of the tasks was in Arthur's house and involved replacing a ceiling and carpentry work. On another farm, three lads had been dispatched to knock down two rundown outbuildings ready for new ones to be built in the spring. Alison explained that the offices were now complete, and a purchasing clerk would be starting on April 1st 2010. He had to work two weeks' notice. I had big plans for future developments and the new purchasing clerk would have a nice smooth run to settle into the job as Ben and Alison had set up all our current requirements, all he had to do was follow suit until the next project started and then he would have his hands full.

Alison also told me that Harry Tooland had been around and she was not sure why. He said he wanted a word with me and would not explain to Alison what it was about. After the meeting I called Harry to see what he wanted me for; to my surprise, he asked if he could come to the house to discuss something. After the call, I sat pondering what he had said and felt uncomfortable about the forthcoming meeting. I arranged for Harry to come at 2 pm and on his arrival met him at the door. We went into my office and Martha brought us coffee and left. I turned to Harry and asked him what was troubling him. He was fidgeting and looked very ill at ease. Harry started by saying how much he had helped me with assisting in ensuring the planning proposal had been accepted and the council meeting had initially been opposed until he had spoken up in its defence. I had a bad feeling that I knew where this was leading. Harry looked me in the eye and stated that if he had not been behind the planning and council meeting and pushed as hard as he did, the proposal would not have been granted. He went on to say that he felt he should be recognised for his efforts and awarded accordingly. The hairs on the back of my neck were more than standing up. I looked Harry in the eye and asked what he had in mind. He suddenly changed to talking about the holiday he had last summer and that he had been looking at a small villa in

Spain but was a little short to purchase it outright. I asked how much he wanted, and he replied seventy thousand pounds looking very much more confident and at ease. Trying to collect my thoughts I told Harry that I would need to think over his request and would come back to him in a couple of days.

I knew our conversation was being recorded and as soon as Harry had left, I went into the little room where all the recording equipment was and replayed our meeting. As it was quite late, I decided to try and sleep on Harry's proposal; it was a restless night. The next morning after talking through the previous night with Julie, I telephoned Robert and asked if he was free to pop over some time. Robert did not have any free time for a couple of days but promised to call me and come over as soon as he could. Two days later, Harry called me to see if I had considered his request. I explained that I had been swamped with work and needed a couple more days and would get to it before the weekend, praying that Robert would free up some time before then.

That evening around 7 pm the buzzer went at the main gate; I was relieved to hear Robert's voice. Robert and I retired to my office, and he immediately asked what was wrong. I simply told Robert what had happened and showed him the video of our conversation. Robert explained that this was not the first case that had cropped up with Harry and I had done the right thing by bringing it to him. Robert asked what I wanted to do, and I explained that I felt appalled by Harry's brazenness and asked Robert what should be done. Robert asked if he could take the tape and five minutes later left. He was a bright colour of red and I knew that he was angrier than I had ever seen him.

Late the next day, Robert called to explain that Harry

had been arrested and the file had been sent to the Criminal Prosecution Service, with Robert's recommendation, and Harry had resigned from the position of Lord Mayor with immediate effect. A week later, Robert called me to let me know that Harry was being investigated for several other concerns of using his position as Lord Mayor to gain financial rewards for himself. It appeared to go deeper and that Harry had implicated several other members of the council on corruption allegations. Robert said that the evidence I had provided had forced Harry to inform on other council officials in order to assist the police. It was not until months later that I was to find out how this had played out. In short, Harry had been found guilty of abusing his position as Lord Major and taking into account his assistance with the police, was given two years imprisonment and banned from holding public office for life. Four other members of the council were also investigated, two of them were arrested and given lighter custodial sentences. Regarding the other two, there was insignificant evidence to warrant legal action against them. However, they both resigned from the council.

William the Gardener had done a fantastic job with the walled garden and kept the household supplied with lettuces, radishes, onions, carrots, parsnips, cabbage, tomatoes, cucumbers, sprouts, cauliflowers and turnips and he had planted two apple trees and one pear tree. He told me that he could not do potatoes as he had run out of ground and they took up too much space. William had OCD and this came to a boiling point one day when his fork had gone missing from his shed. We all started looking for it and William was beside himself. I found it eventually in what had once been a stable block for two horses. Either Danie or Becky had come down for the weekend and used it to clean out the stables as they were talking about having a horse each and had not returned it. I had to warn them both not to incur the wrath of William. They were quite upset to know they had caused him such distress because they treated him almost like a brother.

7

Full steam ahead

It was now coming towards the end of June 2010 and although many parts of the country were suffering from flooding and heavy rainfall, Kent appeared to be getting off lightly. Building work had resumed at a far better pace than anyone had hoped for. Fifty houses were complete and a further fourteen were well under construction. Ben had proved a far better project manager than I could have ever wished for. He took his job to heart and on the odd time we bumped into each other on site, I had to remind him he had a wife. Ben just laughed it off and got his head down and went back to work.

We were starting to struggle to get professional builders and although Ben had done a marvellous job recruiting up to now, we estimated we need twice the workforce we had to grow the business at a better and faster rate. We had twenty-four men on site and Ben's small team and needed as many again; we had to start looking out of the box. Accommodation in the area was limited and what was available, the lads Ben had brought in from outside the area were already using. Bringing in people from afar is fine but it comes with limitations, travelling time being the main one and we had to resolve this problem. After some time, I came up with what I thought may be a solution, hiring a marquee that could be erected on the field not far from the site. We could hire beds etc and put electricity, water and heating in using the generators.

I informed Jonathan of my proposal and asked him to oversee the task. In the meantime, Ben started to work his magic, recruiting from afar with Alison's assistance. By the time the marquee had been erected and furnished, Ben had arranged a further thirty men and women. We set up a small canteen in the marquee to supply everyone with a reasonable meal in the evening and a hot breakfast first thing. It wasn't the Ritz, but at least the lads could get two hot meals a day. In the village, only a short ride away stood an Indian restaurant and a chip shop so everyone had options.

I went into the chip shop one evening to find two lovely ladies behind the counter. I started talking to them and they told me that a new housing estate was being built up the road and that they were worried they would not be able to cope with the new demand. I guess they were normally getting half a dozen customers a night and with the additional builders this had doubled. I wondered how they would cope with the people from a thousand houses, I knew they wouldn't. The first stage was to build two hundred and fifty houses then split off a few of the staff to start on the mall while the rest were to concentrate on stage two, another two hundred and fifty houses.

By October with the extra labour, we were almost at the end of stage one. Impatient as always, I asked Ben if we had the capacity to recruit more labour to send men to do some of the work on the farms and also to push harder on the industrial park. Ben said we had space in the marquee for an additional twenty men or so and then with a shake of his head, he left.

By 2011, the first two hundred and fifty houses were built; we had already sold over two hundred, and on stage two, a further seventy-three off plan, things were going well. In February 2012, I went over to see Arthur to check on how his recovery was going after his accident. The accident happened as he had been feeding wrap onto the combine harvester and it got wrapped around his hand and he had lost two fingers. He said he was lucky as it could have dragged him in and he may have lost more than just a few fingers. Arthur had signed a five-year contract for the farm with an optional annual increase in rental, at my discretion although I had guaranteed that I would not increase the rent on his farm for two years. This was due to the agreement that I made with Arthur not to increase rent for two years for letting me have back some of the acreages he had been renting to a third party. We discussed how the farm was going and Arthur asked about the rebuilding of his barn and the new roof on one of the outbuildings. I explained that these were in hand and expected work to start in July next year on the barn but the outbuilding may have to wait until the following year as others had a more urgent need.

I was thinking of returning home when Emily walked in and started to set the table for dinner. I was about to make my excuses when Arthur said I could not leave until I had sampled Emily's cooking. I don't know about driving home, I didn't think my stomach would fit behind the steering wheel. Emily was a fantastic cook and the food just kept coming and coming, it was almost midnight when I got home.

By October we had reached the point where Stage two was really doing well; the industrial units were over half built with fourteen of them occupied. We had erected eight feet Palisade fencing all the way around the industrial site with key-coded electronic gates at the entrance. Anyone going in or out had a unique code so we could identify individuals and who was on site. We had also set up a security hut at one of the entrances to stage one that had forty-seven cameras spread across stage one and two and the industrial site; not all the cameras were operational yet but the security hut was manned 24/7.

Having discussed with Robert the aspect of monitoring the sites he could not find any reasons not to go ahead as long as they did not cover the children's playgrounds. It was written into the contract that all the potential homeowners and sub-let tenants agreed, that the sale was only available to them and secondary owners if they agreed to participate fully in the security funding. In all the sales and rents we did we only had one objection, sensing trouble, they did not purchase a house. Apart from the one objection, we were thanked for developing a secure environment for the people living there. The security team now consisted of eight men and although it was not yet paying for itself, I had decided that I would continue to fund it until it passed the break-even level that was estimated once stage two and the industrial units were sold or rented out.

We were now three weeks from the Christmas break and the planning officers were on site every day. I felt they had a hidden porta cabin the amount of time they spent on site. To our disappointment, with only three weeks to Christmas, the planning officers had found a massive problem. One of the sold houses not yet moved into complained to the planning officer that they felt the house behind their house was at the wrong angle and the occupants could see into what would be their daughter's bedroom. When they checked they found it was twenty-seven inches out of position and fifteen degrees out of angle. We tried to reason, plead, and beg - anything short of bribery (this I drew the line at) - to get them to change their minds. The houses were built up to roof level and were awaiting windows going in. Down they came and we started all over again.

Ben was in my office and we were both standing facing each other; I was about to give him the biggest bollocking of his life when I realised it was not his fault. I stopped myself and asked Ben to sit down. I told Ben it was my fault as I knew he was putting in a fifteen-hour day; only a few months ago I had reminded him he had a wife at home and to spend some time with her, typical of Ben he had worked harder. I asked him what we should do, he was at a loss. I decided that I would ask Dave to accompany Ben until Christmas and then in the new year Ben was to delegate some of the time and mundane tasks to Dave under his supervision.

Saturday the 14th of December, I had asked Jonathan and Becky plus children, Danie and Jake, Ben his wife Jill, Dave and Alison, Sandra and Martha out for a meal at our local Indian restaurant. I guess being the local main employer made a difference as we never had a problem booking a table even though the restaurant was always full. At this stage, Rebecca had finally moved down some six months ago with Jonathan and the kids, although Jonathan had been down most of that time helping me sort out all manner of things and had been a great asset. Danie and Jake had joined in the last two weeks and were staying with us until they purchased their own home. During the early evening on our way to the restaurant I took a drive through the village and on the way, I noticed the fish and chip shop was closed; not taking much notice, I carried on to have a lovely evening out.

We had just sat down when the two old ladies from the chip shop walked in. I waved them over and asked if they would like to join us. Talib the restaurant owner altered the table for us and we settled down looking through the menu. I was watching Talib during the evening as he had set himself up as front of house. He floated around the restaurant all evening checking that everyone was enjoying their meal and all was to the correct standard. I saw him on several occasions checking the meals as they left the kitchen. During the evening, I started to have a chat with Mandy and Milly the two ladies that owned the chip shop. By now they had realised that I was behind the housing development. I asked how come they were not open on a Friday night. They explained that they were both in their eighties and with the increase in trade felt that they could not cope, they were putting the place up for sale. I must say I felt very guilty and I knew that it was my fault that they were being forced out due to my actions.

We had a lovely evening and left the restaurant around midnight. When we got home, I explained the conversation to Julie that I had had with Mandy and she came up with the solution, buy the chippy and move it to one of the new shops. It had been looking me in the face and I had not seen it. We were a week from shutting down again for Christmas and stages one and two were by and large complete. The ground work on stage three was complete and they were all ready to move over to stage 4. The Mall on stage two was 50% plus complete and half the shops were finished and decorated. There was still lots to do at the mall; the main hall, clubhouse, snooker hall and restaurant were far from finished, although the main structure was in place, we still had a tremendous amount of work to do.

Production shut down, and everyone went home for Christmas. It was time for me to do my calculations on how the spending was going. We were looking forward to Christmas as we had all the family coming down, it would be maddening for two weeks but at least I had my office to escape into. We had a full house: Donna, Leigh and six children some of whom were now adults; Becky and Jonathan and three kids, again one of them an adult, and finally Danie and Jake. HELP! only kidding. I was still trying to get Donna to move down, but I did admit they lived in an idyllic place and had business to conclude before they could consider a move. I was sure it would happen and I wanted it to as soon as possible because I needed them to start taking up the positions within the business. As I have said before, I wanted this to be a family-owned and run business and that would remain my goal until my last breath. I would be talking to everyone during the Christmas period with a view to taking up the positions within the company and moving it forward further than I had managed in just under four years.

The festivities started and the house was full; I had a chance to talk to everyone individually and sort out a number of roles. Jonathan was to be appointed as Operations Manager. Once the entertainment part was complete, Becky was to take over as Entertainment Manager; Danie was to start looking at transforming one of the shops into a dental practice and researching the possibility of having a doctor on site in the same practice for a couple of days a week, as the nearest doctors' surgery was eighteen miles away and the local hospital almost eleven miles away. I had spoken to both Leigh and Jake about roles that may be of interest to them and asked them to consider what we had discussed and come back to me in the new year. Although Donna and Leigh were not due to move down for a few months and still had quite a lot of projects of their own to complete prior to doing so, providing they did decide to move down, it was not an issue I would push as I wanted them to make that decision themselves.

During this time with the house full, it would have been

impossible for Sandra to stay on top of maintaining the housekeeping so I asked her and Martha if they would prefer to have a couple of weeks off or just join us as part of the family. They both jumped at the chance and I stated that they were not to conduct any of their normal duties over the Christmas period. Christmas went really well and everyone enjoyed themselves. The children running around the house made for a blissful bedlam and on several occasions, I retreated into my study for a little peace. The snooker table came into its own and we had a number of competitions; Jake showed us all up and hardly lost a game. In the evenings we all played board games, cards and various other games. It took a mammoth effort to go down to the gym on the two occasions I did use it, but having the house full of family meant I always had company and chatting while you are working out helps take your mind off the pain, well that's the theory anyway. In practice, I left the gym in pain and suffered during the evening on both occasions.

The next morning, I decided to pay a visit to Mandy and Milly's house and see if I could sort something out for them. I stood outside and knocked on the front door and was just about to leave when I saw light coming from the inner door being opened, the look on Milly's face told me they were not expecting visitors. As she opened the door I apologised for the intrusion and said I felt terrible about them having to give up the chip shop and wanted to know if there was anything I could do to make up for it as I felt guilty that my development had caused this. Milly asked me to come through into the back room and before I knew what was happening, I had a cup of tea and a slice of cake put into my lap. Mandy said that it was time for them to pack it in as they were getting older and it was taking its toll. I asked them what they intended to do. Milly said the house had been built in 1851 and they had lived here all their lives and did not really want to move but they felt they had no choice. They would try to sell the house as a business and if that failed, they would try to sell the chip shop equipment. I asked what they thought the equipment was worth and Mandy said they only bought it last year and it cost over seven thousand pounds. I thought about this for a moment and said, what if I take away the chip shop equipment and replace the front window and door with a standard house one and refurbish the front room and I keep the equipment as payment? I would make sure it was decorated to their taste and a new fire installed and we would not exchange a penny. Both Milly and Mandy accepted my offer and I told them I would have to get planning permission; once that was accepted, I would ensure a couple of men would come down to do the work as quickly as possible. It was two hours before I left and when I got outside, I called Peter Jones, asked him to draw up and submit the planning application and then called Ben and asked him to have on standby two good men to do the work.

8

New land

Julie and I were in the sitting room talking with Robert and Kelly on a bright sunny Sunday morning in January just after everyone had returned home after Christmas when Martha came in saying that a Mr Denver Hodge was at the main gate wanting to have a word. I asked Martha if she knew why and she told me that he had a business opportunity to discuss with me and could he have a chat. I asked Martha to buzz him in through the main gate and I would meet him out front. A few minutes later, Mr Hodge pulled up at the front of the house. He stood around six feet four inches and was well built, clean shaven and very smart looking. He drove an old Mustang car that looked from a distance like it was in immaculate condition. I introduced myself and showed him into my office above the garage. Walking over to the garage he told me his name was Denver and he was an American. We had barely sat down when Martha came over with a tray of coffee and cakes.

I asked Denver how I could help him. He said that he owned some land adjoining mine, some seven hundred acres and was planning on returning to the States and wanted to offer me first refusal on it. I asked him why, and he said that he had four tenant farmers and had been told that I treated the farmers well and fairly and as they had been farming the land for three or four generations, he felt that I would show them the same courtesy. He apologised for calling on a Sunday but his return to the States was imminent and also urgent. I asked when his flight was booked for and he said in a fortnight. I said I may be interested but would need to see the property and each farm to assess the condition and its status. He said that should I be free tomorrow he would be happy to accompany me around. I said we would be accompanied by my estate manager, Jonathan, and he said the more the merrier. I asked what price tag he was looking at and he replied six million. I asked why he was returning to the States and could he not come back to the UK after he had sorted out his business. He said that his father had died and he had to return to sort out the estate. He stated that his family lived in Denver and the estate covered four square miles and he had inherited all of it. His only surviving relative was his mother who needed to be looked after.

We chatted a little more and within the hour he said he had taken up enough of my time on a Sunday and prepared to leave. I showed Denver out and straight away called Jonathan to arrange to meet us the next day. Then I returned to the sitting room, apologised to Julie, Robert and Kelly for my absence and settled down to join in their conversation, but my mind was thinking about tomorrow.

The next morning, I met Jonathan at the top of the drive and we decided to go in two cars as Jonathan had another appointment at noon at the site. When we arrived, we realised that we were looking at land on the side of the M62. We met Denver as agreed at 10 am, I introduced Jonathan and we agree to look around the site using just Denver's car as he knew the route he was going to take. While we were driving, I asked him what rate he charged per acre and whether there were any additional charges for the houses and buildings. His acre rate was a little higher than ours at £525 per acre per month and £350 for the houses. For the outbuildings, he charged nothing.

Our first stop was at a Mr Roberts who rented seventy-five acres and did dairy farming. He lived in a three-bedroomed house with his wife and young son. I guessed he was in his forties and farming had been his life having taken over the farm from his parents and grandparents. The farm had been in the family for two hundred years and originally covered almost one thousand acres, but over the years had been sold off. He greeted us and introduced us to his son, Alan. We walked around the farm, into the barn and out building and ended up at the house. The roof of the house needed replacing but the rest was in very good order. The second farm, being 100 acres was run by a chap called Arthur, He again looked in his forties and the farm was agricultural. The barn was used for the storage of farm machinery and all the buildings and house looked in good order. Once again, he and his family had been farming the same land for over one hundred years and had rented it from Mr Roberts's family originally.

The third farm was not so good; Denver told us that the tenant was in arrears with the rent and proving to be a difficult customer. He was reluctant to show us around and only after Denver took him to one side to have a word, did he start to co-operate. In the three-bedroomed house, all the windows needed to be replaced and the barn needed to be taken down and replaced; the outbuildings were ok but needed some T.L.C. His farm was the smallest being only thirty-five acres and he raised pigs.

Finally, we ended up at Martin Tells' farm. He had five hundred acres and did a mixture of dairy and agriculture. He had three barns and several outbuildings all in very good condition. He was a very pleasant chap who welcomed us into his house and introduced us to Brenda his wife, and his three sons, Mark, Luther and John. We were shown around the farm and while Jonathan and Denver were looking over the roof of one of the barns, it gave me the opportunity to talk to Martin. As we walked back to the house, I discovered that it had been Martin who suggested Denver talk to me about selling the estate. My tenants had told him about the set-up I ran and felt that I would treat the tenants fairly. While I was talking to Martin and enjoying a cuppa, Jonathan and Denver walked into the house. I thanked Martin for showing us around and we returned to Denver's car.

When we were driving back to our cars, I asked Denver if any of the farmers had asked to purchase the farms from him rather than be sold as a job lot. Denver said that two of the farmers, Martin and Arthur had both shown interest but, neither had the funds and he heard that I most likely would only look at a job lot. The estate turned out to be seven hundred and ten acres and I estimated its value at around the six million as Denver had suggested. I told Denver that I knew that time was pressing and I would come back to him within three days. He dropped us off at our cars and we bid him good day. I asked Jonathan to call me once he had attended his meeting and update me on any concerns, also to go through what we had seen today, Jonathan said he would pop around that evening and go through it all with me.

I got home at around two pm and went into my office to start making phone calls. I called our solicitors to check out what needed to be done and what they advised about the poor tenant, and Ben, to see what the status was on using some of the men to repair and replace the barn and outbuildings. Finally, I asked Alison to get onto Land Registry and check out the ownership of the land and what may bite us at a later date. I asked her to come back to me as soon as she could with whatever she found. When the report came in from Alison, it did not show anything that gave cause for concern. She had dug deeper and found out that Denver had been in the UK for fifteen years and owned several shops in London as well as the estate he was offering us. His farm/estate in the States had been run by his family for over one hundred years and was well established and very prosperous.

The solicitors called to say they had spoken to Denver's solicitors and Arthur, the difficult tenant, had been a problem for years. They had tried to have him evicted and failed as the farm he rented was his home and business and it got very messy. I asked as we were possibly becoming the new landlord, would this make any difference? They replied that they thought they could get him out but could not guarantee it. I decided to go and see Arthur myself that afternoon and find out what his problem was. I drove down onto his farm and could see the look of surprise on his face when I got out of my car. I did not mince words and after saying hello etc I asked Arthur what his problems were. He told me that Denver had promised to replace the barn and do up the house four years ago and had done nothing since. He said that he started to play up by withholding the rent and being difficult in order to try to get the promised work completed. I told Arthur that should I purchase the estate from Denver, I would replace the barn and do up the house within twelve months. However, should he continue to default with the rent during that period and any period after that, I would see him evicted and no civil rights would prevent it. He said all he wanted was to have what had been promised done.

Ben called me to say that he had still not utilised his own small team fully and could divert three men to do whatever was needed for a few months until phase three of

Millionaire Row went forward. Later that afternoon, Jonathan pulled up outside and we went and sat in the sitting room and talked through the events of the day. Jonathan told me that the ground survey had not shown any surprises and he could not find any public rights of way or anything else. I told him that Alison had looked through Companies House and I explained what she had found regarding Denver's involvement since coming to the UK. I explained that the Ordnance Survey report brought no worrying concerns or infringements that would prevent us from seeking planning permission and if granted, developing the site should we choose to. Having said that, at this stage with steady tenants, I was more inclined to leave it as it was.

The next morning, I telephoned Denver and made an offer of five million pounds, stating the difficult tenant and poor state of the houses and farm buildings. To my surprise, Denver did not argue, he simply said OK, I accept. I told him I would send over new contracts for the tenants and expected him to get them signed and returned to me and invited him to our house the following week on Friday to sign the paperwork and conclude our business after which I would transfer the five million into his account.

With this new acquisition, it would now make our estate well over three thousand acres. Jonathan had been working with the designer for a full week, fine-tuning the plan for the mall at the new site and he came down on Wednesday afternoon to go through it with me. Originally, the supermarket situated at the front of the mall would be 12,000 square feet with a secure rear yard and eight shops on the one side each would be 5,000 square feet with a one-bedroom flat above and at the rear, a small secure yard on each unit and on the other side, sixteen smaller shops each being 3,000 square feet with a storage room on the first floor and a yard and storage space to the rear. I loved the plan and told Jonathan that he had done an excellent job The only change I had stated when I first saw the plans was to site the supermarket at the bottom of the mall; I did not want people coming to the mall walking into the supermarket and once finished their shopping going straight home. In order to give the smaller shops a chance, if the supermarket was at the bottom of the mall, everyone would have to walk past all the other shops to get to it, this would enable the shops to show off what they had available. The only exit at the bottom of the mall was a one-way system for emergency purposes only. Jonathan had said he would see to it and this he had done.

We were still only in the early part of the year and some major changes had taken place with the acquisitions of two farms totalling 1460 acres when another opportunity raised its head. Late that evening, Jonathan phoned to say he had been approached by a chap called Martin Jones. He said that he had land at the far ends of our land bordering the M62 that he wanted to sell and the site was a total of 42 acres. Jonathan had arranged for him and me to go the following morning to view the site. Nine o'clock the next morning, Jonathan picked me up and we drove the few miles to the site; it had been derelict for a number of years and in the middle stood three large, decaying buildings. We met Martin Jones and his two brothers, Donald and Geoff, and walked around the periphery, ending up at the three buildings. While walking around, we discovered that the land had been in the family for a number of years, however, they did not have the funds to develop it. They had heard what we were doing and thought they would give us first refusal. I asked if they had had any problem with Japanese Knotweed or mining issues and they all gave a no response.

I asked what price they were looking at and they stated that they wanted a quick sale and had reduced the price; it was up for £75,000 per acre, a total of £3,150,000. I informed them that we would consider it and get back to them within the next three days.

While Jonathan and I were driving back, we both felt it was too cheap because should it gain planning permission, that land would sell for many thousands more per acre. Before we reached home, I called Alison to start looking at all the normal requirements. I telephoned our solicitor and gave him the coordinates and asked him to start a draft contract. Jonathan stated he would use his contacts to find out what he could regarding the three brothers.

Within the three days, we had a very good insight into our new friends. Robert Barnes had started his own security company obtaining information at a cost on just about anything. He told me that the brothers were into some bad dealings with people they owed a lot of money. The type of people you don't fall behind with payments to as it was likely to get very nasty very quickly. I asked Robert what he felt they owed and he stated around one and a half million. They were into some businesses in London and these were in financial trouble and only a few months – maybe weeks - from going into receivership. Alison found that the last set of mining reports showed that everything was good and the Land Registry stated they owned the land outright.

Armed with what I felt gave us the edge, Jonathan arranged another meeting with them at the site for 10 am the next morning. I had asked our solicitors to draw up the contracts ready to be signed and also requested he accompany us the next day for our meeting; Jonathan would pick him up on the way to picking me up. We arrived on time and Martin and his two brothers were already present.

I thanked them for meeting us and got straight down to business. I stated that due to the short notice and urgency we would only offer two million for the site, however, should they be prepared to wait until we had satisfied ourselves all was ok, and we would revise the offer upwards. With the information we had gained, I knew that they could not afford to wait because either the chaps chasing payment or the receivers would be closing in on them very soon. I also stated that should our offer be accepted and they signed the contract we had brought with us I would transfer the money directly into their account at the end of the day. Martin started to read the contract while his brothers walked around kicking their heels. They had expected to get the asking price and this had clearly disappointed them. Martin said he would go and sit in his car and talk it over with his brothers.

Jonathan, our solicitor and I walked back to Jonathan's car and sat and waited. We had parked our car facing the opposite way to theirs and I could see their heated conversation going on from our side mirror. Twenty minutes later, Martin came over and said he had signed the document. Our solicitor told him that as the land was in all the brothers' names, all three of them needed to sign the sales contract. Martin returned to his car and came back a few minutes later all signed. I shook his hand and informed him I would transfer the money that evening in full. We started to drive back home knowing we had just made our best deal to date. I telephoned Peter Jones and explained what we had done and asked him to come to my house the next day to start looking at the new development.

While we had been dealing with this issue, I had been informed that the smallest tenancy we had that was only half a mile from the one we had just purchased had decided to give up farming altogether. This tenancy was a sub-let to one of the other farms but maintained its independence by paying its rent directly to me. I called the farmer that allowed the sublet and asked if he had any concerns if I took over the small farm. As he had not been paying for the farm, he was happy for me to do so. The next day, Peter came to see me and I explained that I wanted to develop two sites, one on the coordinates I had provided him with the day before and the second was the small farm just freed up. I explained that on the small farm, some fifteen acres, I wanted plans drawing up to site 30 houses, with approximately half an acre of land each. Each house should be different from its neighbour, have at least 5/6 bedrooms and be top of the range. On the other site, I was looking for using the same template as on the first development but expanding it to include 1,200 homes. To say the least, Peter was staggered. I knew that getting the plans drawn up now and submitted to the local authorities for planning permission would reduce the waiting time down after we had completed our current project. As Peter had the drawings and layout of the first project, I knew that it would not take him long to put together a plan and I told him I expected It to be ready on the forty-two acres within two weeks and the other project within six weeks. I bid Peter a good evening and walked into the dining room to a lovely cooked dinner of roast beef, roast potatoes, peas, carrots, cabbage and gravy. Life was good and I felt I had had a good day and accomplished some major transactions.

During dinner, Julie and I sat and discussed our day. We were talking well into the evening and Julie was telling me about the new litter of pups and how cute they were. She had the Blind Society representative coming the following Monday to pick which ones they felt were suitable for training and were bringing back one that had failed. I asked what her plans were for the pup and she said she wanted to keep it but she had been approached by Ben's wife, Jill, who wanted a dog and she had offered her first refusal. I said I was glad as we already had three Labradors and our original dog, Charlie, running around the estate and although they were well behaved, I felt we had enough. Julie also told me that Danie had called and said that she had seen a horse she wanted to buy and stable it here. I said I did not have a problem with that providing it was made clear that it was her responsibility to exercise and care for it. Danie and Jake had purchased their own home some three miles away and Danie was around our house all the time so I knew she would take her responsibility seriously.

Julie and I had moved into the conservatory and were having a drink when we noticed two deer drinking from the pond, I had established some months previously. They did not appear to be put off with the three Labradors only fifty meters away. After a short while, they walked back into the wooded area at the rear of the property and I wondered how they had got through the fence that Dave had installed some time back; that would be something I would need to investigate tomorrow, time allowing. With only Julie and I in the house, it was very quiet and we felt safe and content with our good fortune, not only on the financial side but also our health was good as well.

9

Stages 3/4/5

We had started back at work as planned on the 6th of January, 2012 all guns blazing. Most of the building staff had returned the day before to get settled down into the marquee and I had arranged for the cook to be ready and waiting. Ben had split the staff into two separate groups, half were at the industrial site while the remainder completed the tweaking of any snags on stages one and two and the rest had moved onto stage three. The ground work team were up and running on stage four. The final laying of tarmac was underway on the drives and roads in stages one and two, and all works traffic had been informed not to enter either stage one or two in works vehicles. The CCTV was operational in both stages and had also been sited at the industrial park. On completing the maths on the cost of security, I had to make some alterations. Houses would have to pay £5 per week each equating to a 90 per cent occupation rate of £234,000.00 per annum collectively; industrial units would pay £6 per week for the smaller units and £8 for the larger ones and £10 for the very large ones equating to 90 per cent £15,444.00 per annum and the smaller shops would pay £6 per week and the club, bar, restaurant, hall and snooker club collectively would be paying £5,366.00 per annum. This would have given a total working on 90 per cent capacity of £254,810.00. As it was my intention from the beginning to have this as a non-profitable system, I estimated the wages for six staff working two on at any time, shift system 24/7 would cost security guards being paid £12.50 per hour multiplied by 168 hours per week multiplied by fifty-two weeks of the year would cost £218,400.00 per annum. This would leave £36,410.00 for updates of equipment, and running costs for a small van to transport from site to site.

The feedback from the residents had been surprisingly good, they were guaranteed a patrol man walking around the estate at times during the night, the industrial units would be visited twice a night and the clubs would have security on hand should any issues arise. In addition to this, all areas of concern were covered by CCTV 24/7. In each of the shops and entertainment venues, a panic alarm had been installed and occasional tests would be carried out to test the results. It had been agreed that should an alarm be activated all available or designated staff would flood the area and the current on-duty security guard would make a direct route to the area and take charge. He had a walkie-talkie and mobile phone that should he need further help, he could call for police assistance. Having gone through this in-depth with the crime prevention officer, I felt we had covered as many foreseeable problems that may occur. I had agreed to cover any shortfalls in the running costs of the security system until it was fully up and running with enough people contracted to finance it on its own standing.

We were moving fast with the development of the industrial site and making really good progress on stage four. It was estimated that the ground works on stage four would be completed in another seven weeks and that the mall would be finished by August. Ben had managed to transfer the equipment from the chip shop and it had been installed and was ready to go. Planning permission had been accepted to change Mandy's and Milly's front room back to a living room and Ben had sent two chaps down to do the work. A further forty-eight houses had been sold off plan in stage four and people had started to move into the houses on stage three with only forty-eight not yet built or sold, plus only three houses in stage two were unsold. The industrial units were starting to come available for rental and already we had a waiting list wanting to occupy twenty-seven of them. We left the show home up and running and moved all the sales and paperwork over into the estate agent's shop, along with a mortgage advisor and I intended to keep this going for the duration.

While I was working in my office at home, Martha came in and told me that a Mister Talib Hussain wanted to see me and he was at the main gate. I asked Martha to buzz him in and show him to my study. When Talib arrived, I could see he was impressed with the house and I felt a rise of pride. I asked if he wanted tea or coffee and he asked for a coke. A few minutes later, Martha came in with a tray loaded down with our drinks and cakes and biscuits. Once we were sorted, I asked Talib what I could do for him. He said he understood that one of the buildings in the new mall was going to be a restaurant and he wanted to know more as this could impact his business. I informed him that he was correct but also stated that no final plans had been drawn up. I looked at Talib and tried to read his mind but he was giving nothing away. He then asked if I had anyone in mind to run the restaurant or was the restaurant for sale. I told him no. He then asked if I would consider himself to rent or run it as a manager. I explained that we were just starting to look at sorting the inside out and had as yet not got very far.

I looked at Talib and asked if he would consider a partnership. I said that I would not be selling any of the buildings in the mall but I was open to suggestions as to what to do with the restaurant. The restaurant Talib had in the village was nice but small in comparison to the one in the mall. I said that a 51/49 share would suit me and for my part of the partnership, I would furnish the tables and chairs and decorations and for his part, he would be responsible for the expenses and setting up of the kitchen. If one side of the deal was more expensive than the other, we would divide the cost on a 51/49 ratio. Staffing would be Talib's responsibility and he would have to sign up to the rental agreement that included the security clause as well as the verbal agreement about assisting, should a panic alarm go off. I asked Talib to consider my proposal over the next couple of days and invited him back on Friday to discuss it further. Having Talib as a partner would also ensure he gave it everything. Talib's face shone, I am quite sure that had I had a contract written up he would have signed it there and then. He left my office and I am sure I saw him skipping to his car.

By August the industrial site had been completed and we were well on the way to completing stage three. Foundations and slabs had been poured and passed off by the inspectors in stage four. Leigh, Donna and all six children had moved down and Leigh had set up in one of the larger units in the industrial site as a sprayer of insulated foam roof covering. I approached the Planners and asked if it were possible to use this on the roofs of the industrial unit as it was more environmentally safe and retained more heat. They informed me that I would have to resubmit for an alteration to my current planning proposal and this I did. The added benefits of this type of roof were that it was guaranteed for twenty years against colour fading, degrading and structural strength. As an added bonus he could do a small unit in a day and the larger ones in two. Once done you could walk on the roof one hour later. Colours were optional however I had stuck to green to appease the planning officers. The alterations to the plans were accepted very quickly and I authorised Leigh to start the work. This was just the lift Leigh needed to set his business off to a flying start and it would give him a good portfolio for future work. Some of the roofs were already covered and these Leigh simply recovered on top of the existing roof however, the ones that had not already been covered, he did from scratch and it was amazing how quickly it was completed. I also played with the idea of doing it on the mall's roof but quite quickly changed my mind when I saw the planning officer's face.

I had made arrangements to see one of my neighbours in January but I had to re-organise this due to the workload at the time. We had arranged an appointment in April at his house. He was the owner of the farm of three hundred and fifty acres adjoining my land. At this stage I was only looking at one acre in particular and having driven past it on the way to his house, I confirmed what I expected. It had been used as a dumping site by fly-tippers and it was down a small recess and the main entrance to one of his fields. I arrived at the agreed time of 2 pm and was met by a gentleman I would say in his seventies; he was well built and very broad and stood about 6'2". I introduced myself and he confirmed that he was William Hardcourt. He invited me in and asked if I would like tea or coffee. I settled on tea and we went into his living room to chat.

He introduced me to his wife, Loretta, and we discussed our families and what was happening on my estate and he told me about his farm. He told me that he had expected me to call earlier than now to look over his farm as he thought I wanted to purchase the whole farm. I explained that was not my intention today but I wouldn't rule it out at a later date. I explained that I wanted to purchase just one acre of land by the entrance of one of his fields and explained where it was. He confirmed that he had been having trouble with fly tipping for months and it had cost a fair penny to keep getting it removed. I said if we could come to some arrangement, I wanted to build a garage on the site and move his entrance to one side of the garage. I went on to say that the garage would be manned 24/7 and hopefully this would deter any would-be fly-tippers. We agreed after discussing a figure of six thousand pounds for the one acre and at my cost to move the entrance to his field. I confirmed that this was subject to obtaining planning permission and that I would draw up the plans, submit them to the planning office and get back in touch when I heard anything.

As I was leaving, I turned around to William and asked as a matter of interest, how much did he think his farm was worth? He looked me in the eye and said it was worth as much as he could get for it. I asked him to ponder the question, and the next time we met, maybe he could give me an answer. I knew that William knew exactly what his farm was worth. I found William to be very quick-minded for his age and no one's fool, he had me sussed from the off. I liked Will and his wife and felt comfortable in their company. When I left, I phoned the office I used to produce all the plans needed to date. I spoke to Peter Jones the owner and asked if I could pop in. He had an appointment in one hour but I was more than welcome to arrive at 4.30 pm.

I decided to drop by on the off chance and see how Mandy and Milly were doing. Before I could even knock on the door, it flew open and Milly welcomed me in. I stood in their new living room and I must say it looked fantastic.

They were both over the moon about the work done by the two lads Ben had sent down to make the alterations and then to decorate it. They had drawn every bit of information out of the two lads; they knew all about their families, where they had come from, their holiday plans the lot. I could imagine the guys leaving drained and two stones heavier. I also knew that they would have welcomed the change from working on site and could not have asked for better bosses, and let's face it, in this domain the ladies were the bosses. Lovely but the bosses.

I went in to see Peter at 4.30 having to drag myself out of Mandy's and Milly's home. He was waiting for me when I arrived. I explained what I was looking at and agreed to take him up to see the site and basically sketch it out. He felt that what I was looking at would go through planning quite easily as the nearest petrol station was thirty-five miles away and if you needed tyres and servicing, you had to go all the way into Folkstone. I was requesting plans for a garage, divided into four units each of 2,500 square feet with a small shop of some 2,500 square feet to act as a convenience store and the main office for the paying of petrol, servicing of cars and vans, tyres, and M.O.T station; this would be positioned on one square acre site.

While Peter and I were travelling back to his office, I broached the subject of another idea I had been pondering on. I called it Millionaire's Row. I knew we were only one hour away from London in fair traffic and this could be to our advantage. I had a small farm with the lease coming up for renewal and the tenants had indicated that they wanted out of the farming business due to their age. It was only a smallholding of some fifteen acres on the far reaches of the estate and very close to the main road to London. I explained that I was looking at building a number of houses in a walled and gated community and each house would be in excess of one million pounds. I was looking at six and seven bedroomed houses all with ensuite, double or triple garages, study, living room, large kitchen, separate sitting-rooms, each sitting in half an acre of land. Peter asked if this was part of the plan I had asked him to work on before I had asked him to look at drawing up the plans for the forty-two-acre site. I confirmed that it was and said I had been giving it further thought and wanted to increase the standard and quality of the houses I would like to build there. I could extend the security to include this site and have it monitored on the same basis as the housing estate and industrial units. We had the capacity of cameras and could use the same technology on the gate where everyone had their own code.

Peter liked the idea but had reservations about having up to 30 houses of this type in one community. He said he would give it some thought and come back to me in a few days. I returned home and by now it was starting to get late, Sandra had left for the evening but had left me a plated meal that just needed warming up. It made a nice change with just Julie and me in the house on our own for the evening. We settled down to watch some television, something I had not really done for months and I found myself relaxing for the first time in a very long time since the holiday. I realised that I was thriving on the adrenaline of constantly dealing with one issue after the other. To me, it was a drug that was fuelling me and although I really enjoyed the night at home with Julie, I could not wait to get into the next day's activities.

Talib came to see me the next day and asked if it was ok to discuss my proposal. I welcomed him in and we went into my study. He said that he wanted a 50/50 partnership as he would be running the restaurant using his expertise and experience. I felt that I did not want to lose control over any part of the mall and said I would think it over. When Talib left, I called Jonathan and asked if he could pop in. Within a couple of hours, he walked into my study. I asked him for an update on the farms and in particular the building of the new barn. He explained that the barn was built and awaiting the door to be installed. A few other minor issues were floating around but Jonathan had these under control, I then explained what Talib and I had discussed and Talib's counter-proposal. I went on to say that I was concerned about losing overall control should anything go wrong in the future. Jonathan said that under the circumstances he understood what Talib was requesting and that when a contract was drawn up, it should state that in the event of the relationship falling into an unworkable partnership, one partner could buy the other out, taking into account we owned the premises. Or if that did not satisfy him, simply reject the offer and say no, it was 51/49 or you go alone.

I decided to call Talib the next day and asked him to come and see me. I had decided to stick with my original offer of 51/49 per cent but, I stated that I would not interfere with the running of the restaurant unless it started to run into financial trouble. I could see that Talib was a little disappointed but when I explained that I had no interest in the day-to-day running of the restaurant and it would all be left up to him, he accepted my offer. I stated that I would get the legal team to draw up a contract and send a copy over for his perusal and if happy, add his signature. We discussed the ins and outs of the move and a timing scale. We were quite sure that the new restaurant would, subject to signing the contract be ready for July at the latest.

Talib left and I decided to make my way onto the sites and have a good look around. I had not been on site for several weeks and felt that I needed to reconnect with the development. When I got to the industrial site, I could not get in as I did not have the security code to access the site. I felt like a fool standing there waiting for someone to let me in. I had been waiting for about half an hour watching what was going on all around me when a man and woman started to open the gate. As I walked through, the woman stopped me and told me that I had no right to enter the site and should leave immediately before she called security. Part of me felt elated and the other half frustrated; frustrated, that I could not get in to have a look around but elated that the security measures were working. I left with a red face and made sure I had my own security number ready for the next time.

I noted on a security report I was reading the following week that the lady and gent had reported me to security, on looking at the camera, the security guard had informed them who I was and I think everyone had a good laugh. Making sure I did not have any further security issues I then decided to go and walk through stages one and two. I was delighted that it all looked so good. In one part of the contract all households had signed, it stated that caravans were not allowed to be left outside any house for more than forty-eight hours. I noticed that the grass was starting to go yellow under the one caravan I spotted, and I walked back to the security hut to enquire what had been done. I think I must have frightened the security guard when I explained what I had seen and started to ask questions as to how long it had been there and why it hadn't been reported and moved. He didn't have any answers. I called Dave and asked him to investigate and if needed start to shake the security up a little. I wanted the team to be on the ball and make the occupants of the estate feel safe, not like they were paying for a service that was a waste of time.

Putting on my high vis and safety hat I continued on to stages three and four. To my surprise stage three was well on its way and footing and slabs were already popping up everywhere in stage four. I then walked over to the shops and found Danie in the new Dentistry; she had the whole place kitted out and staff were already booking people in for appointments. She introduced me to the staff and the new dentist and gave me a tour of the unit. I must say I was well impressed. I told her I was looking forward to her financial report at the next board meeting due the following week. I gathered she was not ready, by the look of fear that crossed her face. I knew she would be working on it tonight and it would be ready for next week.

I then went to the estate agent and spoke to the young girl behind the desk. She did not know who I was and I used this to ask lots of questions before I introduced myself. She went a little pale and I assured her that she was doing a fine job and that I found her most helpful and reassuring. I then made my way over to the main mall and found Becky in the pub, no not drinking, she was organising optics and tables and ensuring everything was in place. I asked if she needed any help and she assured me that all was well. I asked if she had any problem with suppliers, and she said that a couple of the big suppliers were being a little off due to the fact we were not letting them set up and run the place. She also said that apart from that, she had several suppliers that could supply all our requirements. Stocks were already on site and she expected to open the doors the following Friday. I thanked her for her gigantic effort as I knew it had not been an easy transition and it had come with many problems that had given herself and Jonathan some sleepless nights. I reminded her to ensure that she had her financial expenditure sheets ready for the meeting next week and got the same look as I did with Danie.

I returned home around six pm feeling good about what I had seen and confident that the girls were stepping up to the plate. Donna had moved down and had settled into a new house on stage one of the developments; Leigh had got his act together and with the boost of the contract for the roofs of the industrial units had been working flat out for weeks. That work was almost at an end but he had secured another contract on a couple of local farms to insulate the walls of their barns and replace the roofs. Donna had started to source suppliers for the shops and had assisted Becky with acquiring crisps and bar snacks. It looked like these would be coming through Donna from now on as it gave her more purchasing power to negotiate better deals and Donna was good at getting good deals. Leigh, Donna's partner had moved into one of the larger units some 10,000 square feet as he had expanded his business to include, landscaping, patios, gardening and fencing. He had Joe, his eldest son, and occasionally, Cash, his second eldest son working with him on a regular basis and had employed a further five men. Until the local authorities that is, what they call adopted the estate, it was our responsibility for the upkeep of the grass and parks etc around all the sites. I had awarded this contract to Leigh and it had given a big boost to his company. He was inundated with work, mainly for patios.

Jake, Danie's partner, had been training to become a fabricator of aluminium frames for windows, doors and conservatories. Jake had also taken on a 10,000 square feet unit and had moved into plastic extrusion moulding in UPVC to make windows, conservatories and composite doors. He now had four people working for him on a full-time basis and was struggling to keep up with demand. I had got him in touch with the office I used for drawing up the plans for the estate and they were currently putting plans in for conservatories on a weekly basis. Both Jake and Leigh had recruited a couple of builders that had moved onto the new estates to assist Leigh in the landscaping of gardens and laying of patios and Jake had employed them for the laying of bases for conservatories; things for both lads were working out well.

The chip shop had opened and Donna had put a manager into the business and a young chap with Downs Syndrome to work in the back preparing potatoes etc. Tony was a smashing lad, always smiling and willing to take on any task requested of him and he fitted into his role like a glove. Donna also had her two eldest daughters working in the chip shop on the evening shift for pocket money. I now had ten members of the family working or connected with the family business and it was all coming together nicely. We were pushing the build as fast as we could, stage four was progressing nicely and we expected to be finished by the end of 2012/early 2013 with the planned development.

Peter had been to see George the other architect and he had drawn up the plans for the garage complex; these had been submitted and given the green light very quickly. I had agreed to purchase one acre of land from William Hardcourt and went over to see him. William gave me a warm welcome and invited me in. Loretta was working in the kitchen and the smell coming out of there was amazing. William and I had been sitting talking all about the developments and general chit-chat when Lorretta came in with a big mug of tea and scones fresh from the oven, this lady could cook. After I had eaten more than I should have,

I asked William if he had given any thought to the proposal of selling off his farm. He told me that he was torn between selling and passing it on to his eldest son. The farm had been in the family for almost three hundred years. He estimated the farm with the house and barns were valued at around three million pounds. His son had moved away five years ago showing no interest in following the family tradition. William had broken down the farm into three units each with one hundred acres and installed three tenant farmers. It had given him and Lorretta a fair income for the past five years but they were beginning to wonder how their future and that of the farm were going to work out. I said I could not make a decision for them it was something they would have to work out for themselves. I spent the next couple of hours sampling more of Lorretta's wonderful scones and left around 9 pm.

By the time I got home the house was in bedlam; we had all the kids and grandchildren running around the house. We all settled in the larger of the two living rooms and chatted until after 11 pm when the children were starting to get tired and I must admit so was I. Julie and I settled down gone midnight that evening and I had to be up early the next morning to attend a council meeting headed up by the new Lord Major. This time a woman had been elected and she was called Lady Lord Mayoress, Brenda Hill. Robert on possibly his last appointment as Chief Constable was in attendance with a full council commitment.

Unbeknownst to me, I was to receive an award from the council for services to the community with the development and expansion of the village. I felt it was a great honour and was surprised how it had all been kept secretive as I tended to hear most of what was going to happen in advance these days. Julie had kept it from me but had known all about it for several weeks. We went home that evening and on our return Dave and Alison were waiting on the doorstep, a bottle of champagne in hand to congratulate me. Of course, I knew that without Julie at my side, none of this would have been possible.

While Julie and Alison sat in the living room talking and watching television, Dave and I were playing snooker; it had only been the third or fourth time that Dave and I had managed to use the table. Later that night Dave and Alison settled down at our house in one of the guest rooms and Julie and I retired around 2 am. Everything I could have hoped for was coming together and I felt like the luckiest man in the world.

At the end of December 2012 we shut down for the annual Christmas holidays. Stage three was complete and stage four was not far behind and with only five houses left to sell on stage three. Forty per cent of stage four had been sold off plan and a further 125 had been sold of those completed. The garage built on what was William Hardcourt's land was having the ground work conducted and it would not be long before construction would start. It was expected to be complete by the end of March. On the industrial site, all but two of the units were occupied. It felt like the past five and a half years had been hard but extremely rewarding.

Julie and I spent Christmas at home with most of the family staying over as well. Knowing that Martha and Sandra were going to spend Christmas on their own, I asked if they would like to stay over Christmas as they did the year before and they both jumped at the opportunity. I agreed that it was on the condition that Sandra did not go into the kitchen and Martha did not do any housework. It was only the second time we had ever had the house full and it again felt like a true home. Everyone did their part to ensure Christmas went off smoothly and keep Martha and Sandra from getting into cooking and housework. I had had the company accounts done on an annual basis as the law required and submitted to HMRC, but I felt it was time to put some basic figures together for myself and the family to have an understanding of how the finances stood. At the end of the day, I had spent a lot of money building up the estate, the projects I had developed and those that had not even started yet.

10

Financial standing

To date I had spent 20 million on the house, a further 7 million on new land, 10 million on ground works 75 million on materials, legal work, planning, architects and incidentals, a total of £112,000,000.

On the positive side, we had sold 693 of the 1,000 houses at an average of £250,000 each, bringing in £173,250,000. We were already starting to bring in rent from the industrial site and some of the shops but taking the main figures into account, we were in profit of £61,000,000 with a further 307 houses to sell and rents to come in. I also knew that I would need to spend a further £38,000,000 to finish the current project but that would bring in a further £76,000,000. We would own the house, industrial park, the shops, garage, entertainment centre, office and garage complex and over 4,500 acres of land all estimated in excess of £ 64,000,000. Bottom line, our £117,000,000 Lotto win had increased to in excess of £200,000,000 plus £64,000,000 assets. With all the hard work and the right people supporting me, the past few years had proved very rewarding. I had heard it said that to make money you had to have money. Well, I think that this proved the case. At the height of the building works we were employing almost one hundred people, although most were self-employed only twenty-one were employed directly by our company.

We had another project that we needed to start getting our heads around and I gave the family the basics of what was to come in the new developments.

11

Breach of security

Wednesday morning, we all got up late. Becky and Jonathan had stayed over with the grandchildren and we had been woken up by them jumping onto our bed using it as a trampoline. I had a call from Dave telling me that over the weekend the site had been broken into through the fence at the far end and some of the materials had been stolen. This was only the second time we had experienced a breach of security in five years and I was eager to stamp on it before it got out of control. All sites have some theft, a few bricks, a bag of cement, plaster, paint, wood etc, but this was different, they had come from the outside and my gut was telling me they would not stop at what they had taken. I asked Ben if anyone had looked through the cameras and had the security team seen anything. The cameras had picked up two men dressed in black going from house to house on the houses not complete in phase three, collecting what they could carry. They could not get a vehicle close to where they were working so everything they took had to be carried back to their van. We could not see the registration plate but through Ben, we had a good idea of who they were.

I asked Dave to organise a couple of chaps to set up a watch for the next week or two to see if we could put this to bed. Dave organised two of the off-duty security guards to keep an eye open from the not completed houses, sited in phase four. Three days later I had a phone call from Dave at six-thirty in the morning telling me that the chaps and he had caught them red-handed trying to take plasterboard through the eight feet fencing and load it into their van. He had taken them down to the local police station and handed them over. He told me they tried to drive off and had run into one of the JCB diggers. When I saw the van with the bucket of the digger going through the roof of the van almost touching the ground, I did wonder. They were a couple of local lads that Ben refused to hire as he knew they were trouble and light-fingered. Yet again his local knowledge came into use.

A few weeks later, I was told that they had received, due to their previous record, three months imprisonment suspended for two years and 180 hours of community service. We had a few things going on in the completed and uncompleted estate, sheds being broken into, bikes being taken, small but annoying incidents all the same. This was twice the security cameras had proven their worth and confirmed to me that my initial investment had been right. After these two were held accountable the petty stealing and theft stopped. Because three of the security guards lived on the estate, word soon got around how the measures we had put in had justified the five pounds a week each house, was paying for security. We had also had a couple of break-ins through the outer perimeter fence at the industrial site, only for the security to show up and the would-be thieves to run off.

Fortunately, the security team had not been affected by the flu virus that had been going around and had carried on as if nothing had changed. I had not been made aware of this until this incident but, six months earlier a young girl had been attacked right by where the hall was being built; fortunately, again the security hut was only one hundred yards away and hearing her scream, the guards had gone down to investigate. This had prevented what could have been a very nasty attack and although the girl was shaken up and taken to hospital, she was released several hours later. The sites were covered 24/7 with one guard during the day and two guards at night. Should anyone be off sick or on holiday, the extra guard off nights would cover. As an extra backup, Dave would fill in if the need arose, this had not as yet been the case. The plan we had introduced for the snooker club, restaurant, clubhouse and function room should any trouble occur, worked well. On only one occasion due to a little too much drink did we have a ruckus and this was dealt with quickly and efficiently; most people in the snooker club where it had occurred were not even aware something had kicked off. When the security guard arrived, the chap involved had gone home and everything had returned to normal, the security Guard's response time had been seven minutes as he had been down at the industrial site and it was just before shift change over; I thought it had been a fair response.

A television crew came onto the estate one day to see what the reaction to the camera system was. I thought they were going to use it as a breach of privacy and an invasion of civil rights. This was just after the two chaps had been arrested and I guess they picked the story up from the court proceedings. They were talking to the residents and not getting the story they wanted as everyone was praising the system when the security guard turned up with Dave in tow. The guard had called Dave having received a complaint from one of the residents about the film crew's approach and they both confronted the film crew and asked them to leave. Jonathan telephoned the television studio and offered to give an interview on camera and the studio sent a team down to do a short story. Three days later, Jonathan was on national television explaining the advantages of the heightened security measures we had installed and giving a financial breakdown of the costs to each resident. Before we knew it, we were being called from all over the world with requests for information about security and the pavement system we had installed. I telephoned Justin to let him know that the cat was out of the bag about the pavement system and he told me that they had already been advised and it did not change anything as far as they were concerned. Jonathan was offered several jobs as a consultant regarding the installation and set-up of similar systems in several countries and managed to earn himself a nice little packet as a consultant.

We had fifty-seven cameras set up covering the housing estates, the mall, the garage and industrial estate and the footage was downloaded onto disc at the end of each shift and secured should the need ever arise. I had a further fifteen cameras at home, although these were on a separate system and overwritten every thirty-one days and I had the option to download these onto disc as I had done for Robert when I had that issue with Harry Tooland. The costs of security to the residents had built up with a surplus of funds and as I was determined that it remain non-profit making and did not want to start reducing residents' fees or returning a couple of quid, I had asked Dave to increase the number of guards from seven to nine so an extra presence could be felt in all areas over the weekends.

We were in the development of creating a car wash plant next to the garage as we had a little bit of land left over from the build when Leigh said that there was more money to be made setting up a non-automated car wash and the process was quicker being done by hand than the traditional drive-through car wash. We were in the process of purchasing an automated system but listening to what Leigh was saying and realised it made more sense and it would create employment for a couple of local lads. As we had only got as far as laying the drainage and connecting it up and the concrete base, we could quite easily change direction and cancel the new plant. With the automated system, it would use more water and take longer and some of it would require input from the car owner. With what Leigh had suggested, the owner of the car would stay in the car or take a seat in the office while the work was completed for them unless it was a question of valeting the car. For this, we had to build a small sitting area where the owner could sit and wait for the car to be done.

The trade at the garage was flying, services for cars were booked months in advance, tyres and the M.O.T. bay were constantly busy and the shop on top of petrol sales was taking £11,000 a week. We were the only petrol station in thirty-five miles so we almost had a captive clientele, and this brought in the other business that was making the garage a real success. We added another two cameras to the system covering the car wash just in case. I asked the manager of the complex to interview anyone interested in working at the car wash and he was inundated with applications. It was up and running within two weeks and became extremely popular, bringing in an additional profit of £5,000 per week. The security were frequent visitors to the garage as it had a nice coffee machine and often pulled in for a chat as well. The presence of security on site also deterred any would-be thieves and I was happy for them to have a coffee as long as they did not take advantage and spent too long in any one site. The idea was that they were seen to be everywhere, and with the expansion of the sites and wanting them to also do walkarounds, they needed to keep on the move.

In all the time we had had the security up and running

we had never had any serious issues with the security guards themselves. It helped that three of them came from the housing estate and five of them were ex-military. I had made it plain to Dave that where possible I wanted former military personnel working for us as I felt they had the discipline and self-drive to use their initiative when required. Apart from the occasional drunk trying to find his or her way home, the security had quite a cushy number and could become a little worrying when down at the industrial site late at night, but often someone would be working in one of the units and it gave a little reassurance to know that someone else was around, plus they were in constant contact with their main office with the walkie talkies and could be seen just about anywhere on the security cameras.

The cost of security had increased since I asked that a further two men be employed and I was prepared to foot the cost myself until the houses and the industrial units were all sold or rented out. With some of the surplus money available I purchased additional walkie-talkies for each of the shops and larger entertainment units, this was so they had direct communication with the mobile security should an incident occur and they could be on the scene much quicker. Once all the houses were sold, the security finances would be self-funding. However, until then if needed, I would give an interest-free loan to the security fund re-payable once it became self-sufficient. Allowing a 5% shortfall for empty houses and units etc, the security charge would still generate £243,393.80 and would cost £218,400 plus the running of the security van.

By now we were approaching Christmas again and I must say the time had flown. All our current projects were almost complete and the labour force had been reduced to just Ben's team and a couple of dozen additional men finishing off odd jobs. The entertainment centre was up and running and proving to be very popular; the garage complex had services, tyres, MOT, fuel and car washing and the service department was booked for months in advance, it was proving to be a good earner. With just three weeks till Christmas, I had a telephone call from Peter Jones our architect telling me that both projects had been given full planning permission and the green light to proceed. I thanked Peter for all the work he had done in getting the plans together and pushing where possible the development through.

I had been looking forward to Christmas but now felt the knot in my stomach and knew that my mind would be racing with plans during the festive season. I called a meeting with Jonathan, Ben, Dave and the girls and Alison to take the minute to pass on the good news and asked them to start getting their heads around the forthcoming projects. The marquee was due to be dismantled and the ground it stood on was going to be a building yard and the other half a garden centre. I asked Jonathan to organise getting it partitioned and fitted out and to order a larger marquee for the next project and as soon as possible after Christmas, get it erected. I asked Dave to organise fencing up on what would be the first phase and a second fence around where Jonathan would be putting the marquee. I asked Ben to work with Alison and our purchasing clerk to start ordering materials and give notice to the ground crew hopefully to start work in January.

The volumes of materials would be staggering and once they started to arrive, Ben would need to talk to Dave to arrange security. Most of the heavy plant equipment had been moved back to the security of the industrial site and although we did not have any units available to put them in, at least it was secure within the compound. Ben explained that the area he would need to store the raw materials would be extensive as just basic standard brick he would need around eighteen million alone however, these would not be delivered all at once and he would call them off as required. But this was just one material and by the time the others were purchased, he suggested making a secure area on what would be area five or six as these would be the last part of the project to be started. Jonathan stated that a small field stood next to the project and suggested hiring it and using that for the marquee and security of materials, this way nothing would impede the progress or development. That being the best suggestion we all agreed and the meeting was adjourned.

Just after lunch, I had a phone call from Justin congratulating me on the new project. We had a couple of small things to change, but by and large, the entire plan had been granted. Again, I felt that Jonathan working tirelessly with Justin had made a huge difference. The estimated costs for ground works, labour, materials and land were 245 million pounds with a potential profit of 195 million pounds spread over three years. We knew that the location of Millionaire Row and the new site for the 1200 new homes being built within commuting distance of London, would bring premium prices. Ben had done a marvellous job on the last project in keeping our stocks high but we knew that obtaining the basic raw materials now would be difficult in the volumes we required.

I had asked Ben to make the phone calls before Christmas if that was possible, to put our suppliers on notice of the volumes we would be requiring. We had enough materials to cover any requirements on any of the farm houses, barns, out-buildings, and houses on the estate but the new build was another matter.

As we were again coming to Christmas, Julie and I had hoped to get away for another holiday before the mad rush of the new development kicked in. Unfortunately, with all the new developments planning we gave up looking for anything. It was too late for the family to change plans of what they had organised for Christmas and as we were now not going away, Julie and I spent the week going around Becky's and Danie's homes. Donna and her crowd had booked to go away for the two-week break and both Julie and I were envious that they were getting plenty of sun. They had gone back to the South of France where they had purchased a second home. Even at this time of year, they were getting weather in the mid-twenties. Twice we stayed over, once at Becky's and then at Danie's house as it had been getting late. Martha and Brenda had stayed at our house over the Christmas period with our blessing and I felt guilty as for the past three years we had all been around, they must have found it very quiet without all the crowd.

12

London

We had just finished our monthly board meeting in January and were all sitting around having a general chat when the phone rang and Donna said it was Justin. I took the phone and asked how he and the family were and he told me that they were all well and complaining he was working too hard. I said it was the price of high office and getting on in life. He was working flat out on one thing or the other and he had been stopped in his tracks due to something I had done. He went on to say that the development and ground works I had incorporated in the plans for the building of the housing estate had gained the interest of some officials in London and he wanted me to go there and update some of his colleagues on the pros and cons. I attempted to get a little more out of Justin and all he would say was that it was a little informal meeting to see how the development had gone. I said I would bring Jonathan with me as we had both worked on the idea together. Justin congratulated us on securing the second building site and wished us good luck.

I arranged to go to London the following Monday taking Julie, Jonathan and Becky with the plan to make a few days of it and enjoy the sights of London and take in a couple of shows. I asked Dave to take us all to the train station on Saturday morning so that we could get settled into the hotel before our meeting on Monday and also as parking in London is always a problem and most of the sites were within a short distance of the hotel, we would not need a car. We arrived in London at 11.46 and a few minutes later and a very short taxi ride arrived at the hotel. While Julie and Becky were booking us in, I took the opportunity to call Justin to let him know we had arrived. He told me that a car would pick Jonathan and me up at 10 am Monday and drive us directly to the meeting.

That evening we went to one of the West End shows and afterwards went for a meal at a restaurant all within walking distance of the hotel. On Sunday, we got up early and by nine am were breakfasted and ready to go. We visited the London Eye, I did not realise the height of the wheel and as I do not like heights, I left fingerprint marks on the rails and could not wait to get down. Once we were down, I realised that it was quite a nice experience and would be quite happy to go on it again. Madame Tussauds was ok, and the underground bit where they try to frighten the life out of you was brilliant. We then went on a trip up the River Thames; this took up the rest of the afternoon and at one point we all got off for a walk around and had fish and chips from a mobile chip shop. Once we returned to our hotel, we had time for a couple of hours of relaxation before we went out for our evening meal. We decided to go to a steak house and both Jonathan and I had the largest steak I have ever seen. I have to admit I could not manage all mine but Jonathan cleared his plate.

The next morning at 10 am Jonathan and I were standing outside the hotel and a black, chauffeur-driven car pulled up and invited us to get in. Withing ten minutes, to our utter surprise, we were pulling into Downing Street. The police at the main gates checked who we were and allowed us to enter and the car proceeded to pull up at Number Ten. Both Jonathan and I were in shock, neither of us expected this and having taken Justin at his word that it was an informal meeting, neither Jonathan nor I were in our best clothes. We entered Number Ten and were again checked by security when Justin came out of a side room to show us where to go and explained that several people had expressed interest in the initial groundwork that I had constructed and wanted to discuss it further. I think both Jonathan and I must have looked like rabbits in headlights. I said to Justin that he could have given us the heads-up about where the meeting was to take place, and he just smiled and said it was all to do with security. We were shown into a room with a massive oval table and very comfortable chairs. We were the only ones present in the room at this stage and Justin explained that we would be joined shortly by several people. Five minutes later, people started to enter. Justin had popped out and Jonathan and I did not know whether to stand or stay seated when these people came in.

Finally, Justin came in with the Prime Minister and they took a seat. The PM opened the meeting by thanking Jonathan and me for coming at such short notice and introducing the people around the table. Jonathan and I were seated next to Justin and the PM next to him, following around the table were Minister for the Environment, Donald Toute, Transport Reginal Hunt, Energy Angela Heart, Housing, Justin, Treasury Brendan Stone and a couple of others that I could not remember their names, were introduced that were there to take the minutes and act as advisors after the meeting.

As Justin had given us a basic understanding of why we were there, I had brought plans and drawings of the blueprints of the estate with a hard copy of a spread sheet explaining several long-term benefits and savings and realised the importance of this meeting, I apologised for not being better prepared. The PM waved away my apology and told me they were in my debt for coming to show them what we had done. I had questions fired at me from every direction, wanting to gain a better understanding of each phase, the costings involved, and what I thought would be involved in introducing it into housing estates that were already built. What difficulties we faced, and why we had done it this way or that way, the questions went on for several hours. Drawing the meeting to a conclusion, the PM again thanked us for our time and explained that we had given them plenty to think about. He asked if we were prepared to give a series of presentations and if needed, advice and guidance should any of the ideas we had discussed be implemented. Both Jonathan and I stuttered a yes, and at that the meeting was over.

As if by magic, the doors opened and a couple of platters of sandwiches were brought in followed by tea and coffee, a series of informal discussions took place and the PM asked me about the housing estate and what we had been doing. I was shocked to find out that he knew so much and realised that Justin must have filled him in before our meeting. He knew all about the security cameras, and security guards in the lot. Half an hour later, everyone left the room leaving Jonathan and me alone and feeling drained. Justin returned and told us that the PM was very impressed with what we had achieved and had asked the Treasury to conduct a report on the financial cost and potential long-term savings, he also asked the Energy and Environment Secretaries to look at it from their perspective and draw up potential benefits. We were then shown out of Number Ten and driven back to our hotel. Although it had been an intensive several hours, both Jonathan and I were elated and thrilled by the experience and could not wait to tell Julie and Becky what had happened.

Before leaving Number Ten, Justin had arranged to pick

us all up at the hotel at eight pm and take us to a club. We had tickets for another show and we managed to get the tickets altered to the next day for the afternoon showing so we decided to stay on an extra day and make it a long weekend. We were limited in time as the meeting had taken longer than we expected and at six o'clock we went to an Indian a short walk away for our evening meal. We returned at seven-thirty, just in time to freshen up ready for Justin to pick us up. He arrived a couple of minutes later in his official, chauffeur-driven car to take us to his club.

The car pulled up outside what I thought was a large, back door, two huge chaps were standing on either side and as we arrived, one of them came forward and opened the door. As we all got out and walked to the large door it opened and we were all invited in. Justin led the way and was clearly known by all the staff. To say the place was plush would have been an understatement; the carpet felt like you were floating and the wallpaper and lighting were extravagant, to say the least. The lighting was subdued and we were shown to a table; all the tables were arranged so that anyone seated would be able to see the stage. The club was packed and a woman was onstage singing as we arrived. A young lady presented us with a menu for cocktails and took our order. Justin must have seen that we were all a little shell-shocked and explained that this was his local while away from home and that it was members and members' guests only. Our drinks arrived and we settled in to watch the show.

Jonathan and Justin were in deep conversation and that allowed me to watch the show. After the lady had finished singing, she was followed by a magician/pickpocket, he asked for members of the audience to join him on stage and as they walked onto the stage, he picked out a mini vibrator from a lady's pocket to her embarrassment and took every watch, ring and wallet without anyone having a clue from all on stage. He showed how easy it would be to lose your valuables and not have any idea it was missing until you needed them. The audience was in fits of laughter throughout his performance.

Next up was a ventriloquist who used members of the audience instead of dummies. He stood behind the people on stage and used his voice to make it look like they were talking to the audience. Finally, a Hypnotist act was the last act of the night and he again asked members of the audience to join him on stage. I was so glad that our table was not at the front. Eight people were sitting on stage and he told them they were unable to get up off the chair. He told them that they all had X-ray vision and could see all the beautiful ladies and gentlemen in the audience naked. He went on telling his victims they were washing machines, air raid sirens and lots of other things. The audience was in uproar with laughter at the antics performed by the victims of the hypnotist.

We had a wonderful evening and were all sad when it came to an end; having said that, it was four am. We returned to the hotel in Justin's governmental car and invited him to join us at the bar for a nightcap. He told us he was due at a meeting at nine the next morning so wished us a good morning. He thanked us for coming and told us he would keep us informed of any developments regarding the meeting we had at Number Ten. We thanked him for a brilliant evening and said good night/morning.

The next morning, we were up late and only had time for a snack before the show. We were five minutes late getting there, to the disappointment of the audience members having to stand up to let us get to our seats. The show was fantastic and when we got back to our hotel, I think all of us wanted the weekend to go on forever. We arranged for a taxi to pick us up and just had time to finish packing our last few items of clothing before we were told it was waiting outside. We were booked on the seven-thirty train and by nine fifteen we were climbing into the back of Dave's car, all feeling tired but over the moon with the experience of the weekend and some stories to tell to the family, including our visit to Number Ten. Although it was almost ten o'clock by the time we got home, the grandchildren, Suranne, Nina, and Lottie were up awaiting the return of Jonathan and Becky.

14

Second development

January 5th, 2014, a new year and I telephoned Jonathan and Ben and asked them both to come to my office the next day. At nine o'clock the next morning both Jonathan and Ben arrived at the same time and walked into my office. I asked if they were both ready for a new challenge and they said they looking forward to it. I knew that Ben had put everything into the previous developments and would not want him to take this challenge again on his own; thankfully this time he would have Jonathan right at his side from the beginning sharing the pressures. This time Jonathan would project manage the development so that Ben could concentrate on overseeing the workforce and building work. Instead of directing my questions to Ben, I would now ask the question and see who would answer, that way I understood who took responsibility for that part of the programme. It appeared to work well. I asked about the ground work team we hired the last time and Ben stated that he had made the calls before Christmas and that the entire ground work team were available and would be on site and working by the 9th. Jonathan said he would assist Ben in starting to order raw materials in, as the volumes would be staggering and we did not want the development stopped or slowed down because of shortages. Jonathan was also going to organise the security on the outer perimeter fencing working with Dave whom he had already spoken to.

Things were moving fast. Ben had arranged for the ground workers to return sooner than I had hoped for. On the last project, we had to wait for them to become free from previous jobs. Jonathan had already moved our equipment onto the new development site and rented the 3-acre field. Jake had jumped at the opportunity when it arose and had taken on a second unit on the industrial site to increase production on UPVC windows and Jonathan had told him to start producing large quantities of doors and conservatories in readiness for the development. We would require around 132,200 windows and 22,000 outer doors plus an unknown quantity of conservatories. What we had done with the old marquee was to divide it in half, so it was 50/50 in each half of the site. We used this as the garden centre and builders' yard inside space. This came with added bonuses, as it was not a solid construction it was considered rate free.

To develop the garden centre, I advertised for a garden centre manager and a building yard manager and wanted them to start as soon as possible as I wanted them to be involved with its development from an early stage. I had asked Alison to conduct the interviews and reduce them down to what she considered the best candidates. Within a week, she had three potential managers and between us, we decided on a Mr Brian Gold. One of the other candidates called Jacob Dhillon was perfect for the builders' yard; we offered him the position and he accepted it. Brian had been working in gardening all his life since leaving school at sixteen and Jacob had been a roofer working on our site for the past three years and fancied a change.

I had taken Brian and Jason over to the sites and explained what I required them to arrange. I had purchased one forklift truck between the garden centre and builders' yard for them to share as the garden centre would not need a truck for more than a few hours per week and made Jacob ultimately responsible for it. I asked Brian and Jacob to look at what they felt was needed and to organise it within the budget I had set. Brian's first task had been to arrange the construction of the polytunnels and set out how he felt the site should be laid out. I wanted to see his version prior to implementing it and Ben needed to see where he was going to put the polytunnels prior to laying the concrete base. Jacob needed to gather his suppliers' list and for help, he could use the ones we had been using, this would also keep the costs down. The quantities we had ordered over the past few years guaranteed we had the best possible prices anyone could expect to get. Any purchases they made would be placed through Alison initially until the centre was up and running; by then, Brian and Jacob would have their own autonomy and be expected to run the operation in its entirety.

Because the marquee site had been altered by not having to construct the brick-built unit, we initially envisaged and estimated it would be ready within six weeks and the builders' yard would be the same. I told them both that I had wanted the sites open for business by the end of July and this they succeeded in doing and it had now been running for eighteen months. Recruitment had been done through Alison down to a couple of candidates and then final interviews by Jacob and Brian, for the final decision, and Alison would organise contracts of employment. This left Ben with the job of having to get the concrete bases laid in rapid time and the electrics etc into place. Ben said he would do the piping and electrics and plumbing and have it in by the end of May giving both Jacob and Brian a further four weeks to fulfil their targets. Jonathan had taken on the task of purchasing another marquee for the new site and had decided to install a full working kitchen so that the workers could have a good breakfast and evening meal. The current kitchen from the marquee would not be adequate for the new one, however, Talib had purchased new kitchen equipment for the restaurant so the old equipment was still available and added to what we already had, serviced nicely. They would also be able to purchase sandwiches from the kitchen during the day. If they wanted a change, they could always drive up to the first development and then had the option of the chippy or Indian restaurant.

When we had discussed the food that would be served for our workforce, I had insisted that it should be value for money and when viewing the menu, I know that the menu for the marquee would satisfy most of the chaps. For a very reasonable price, you could have a three-course meal and have change from ten pounds. I charged a small fee to stay in the marquee as I was only interested in covering the costs. Ben had already put out the word for staff for the development and had received a very good response. He estimated that he could be close to one hundred workers within two months. We had reduced the existing workforce to just thirty-five men in total for the entire organisation of the building project as we were expecting to be finalising the last phase. We did not want to take on any more staff until the ground workers were near the end of the first phase.

We had put into the plans that the roof of the mall and again the industrial units would be covered with Leigh's foam in the same colour as we had used on the industrial site of the first development. When we first suggested this on the first development, it had been frowned upon by the planners and architects alike. Now we had this on the industrial units we had something to show them and this had gone a long way to making it more acceptable.

Within three weeks, the first stage of the new

development was starting to take shape. Because I wanted the services to run under the paths, laying out the site and the order in which it was constructed altered from the traditional method. This felt odd to some of the new chaps working for us for the first time, but those that had been with us before just carried on as if it was normal. One of the main changes was that the road had to be in place prior to the houses being started. The roads were not a finished project and a lot had to be completed, but it was more advanced than normal with many gaps covered with steel plates to allow the vehicles access to cross from one section to another. Within twelve months, the first houses were finished and set up as the show home and staff from the estate agents on development one were brought down to man it.

Leigh was given the contract of landscaping the garden around each phase as they became available and would also be responsible for its upkeep until the individual houses were sold and the estate adopted by the local authorities. The estate agent's office on development one was to be closed altogether and rented out as we already had a tenant and it was to become a pet shop. Over fifty of the new houses had been sold off plan before work had barely started, and we were getting enquiries regarding the shops in what would be the new mall almost on a daily basis. By late February, the work team had grown to almost eighty-five people, and Ben had recruited most of the staff he would need to finish off the development, although this would take at least two years. As the ground work team moved over to phase two, Ben's team moved onto phase one, this is how it would work until all phases were complete.

We had decided as a collective not to install the security system on the new phase only on Millionaire Row. Our reasons were that it was very expensive and would need constant monitoring. Unless we created a company to oversee security on all sites, we would not have the time to devote to its running. The word got out that we had decided not to introduce the security system and a week later, I received a phone call from a security consultant. He asked if he could come and see me the following day to discuss a proposal. I agreed and at eleven o'clock the next morning a mister Green called. He said he was developing his business and asked if I would be interested in selling the security from the first development and the second. I explained that it was a non-profit making operation and I could not see how he would make money from it as I had guaranteed it would not be set up to make money. He said that the operation on development two he felt could be charged at a higher rate and although the accounts from the first development showed the account was only just in the black, he felt he could draw more money in from the second development to make it worthwhile. He went on to say that as the second development was within commuting distance from London, many of the purchasers would be from there. He felt that for the unquiet system, Londoners would pay much more.

I had to admit, I was impressed with Mr Green's suggestions and said I would seriously think over his proposal. When he had gone, I telephoned Dave and asked him to pop in and see me. He had been over in Alison's office and said he would be with me in a few moments. Dave arrived and I asked him to prepare a financial costing of developing the security system, like for like, as we did on the first development The process would follow the same format we had used during the first development. Dave gave some concerns and stated we had agreed not to introduce the system during this development. I told Dave about the conversation I had just had and said that the long-term monitoring and managing of the security had concerned me as we were not in the business of security. As I had made Dave head of security, I think he felt that this could be his death warrant. I could read Dave's mind and went on to say that I wanted him to take up a new role within the company as an assistant to Jonathan overseeing the farm estates but needed to get this sorted out first. Jonathan had too much on his plate and I felt that he needed an assistant.

Dave and I took the opportunity to have a couple of games of snooker before Dave shot off to start working on his costings. Now the ground work was completed on phase one, Ben would start his team working on the development, The ground workers would complete all seven phases by the end of 2015. Ben had already started with phase one and was preparing to start on phases two and three, the industrial park. Then move on to phase four the shopping mall and then onto phases five and six and seven. The final phase was Millionaire Row and that should be complete by late 2017 or at the latest, 2018.

Ben had placed orders for huge volumes of materials and from the start, although we were given priority from most of our suppliers, we were struggling to get materials in any great volume at this early stage and Ben and I felt it would have an impact on our schedule and finish date. We still had a reasonable volume of materials trickling in but were struggling for plasterboard for the inner walls of the houses and to some degree basic cement. Although we had not stopped or slowed down, we were working hand to mouth and it was giving us some major concerns. The cost of basic materials had started to go up in unprecedented increases and thankfully we had secured contracts with our main suppliers. It was these that were concerning us as although we had not had supplies stopped, it was getting close. I set up a number of meetings with each of the large suppliers and the response was poor. Without exception, they all said that the circumstances were out of their control. They could not get raw materials and if they did manage, they didn't have the labour. We asked what they had in stock and in all cases agreed to take the entire stock at a premium rate.

15

Development two, Fire, Fire

While we were attending the meeting, Jonathan received a call from Ben at the site, he told Jonathan that house forty-seven had just gone up in flames and the fire brigade was in attendance. The building was at the stage where it had the roof almost complete and windows were just about to be put in. From what we could gather, one of the chippies doing the flooring had gone for his dinner and left a heater on a pile of wood and shavings. It had caught fire and by the time he returned, the fire brigade was working on putting out the flames. Both Jonathan and I arrived several hours later to find the site in darkness and no one to be seen. I called Ben and asked him for an update. Ben stated that the chippy had used his own heater as the conditions were cold and that was not pac-tested or permitted on site. He meant to switch it off when he went for lunch and forgot. Ben had sacked the chap on the spot and told him he would hear more about it at a later date. Ben had taken him back to the marquee to pack his stuff and escorted him off-site. I asked Ben what would be the next step. Ben said that the police, fire brigade and possibly the health and safety executive would want to conduct a full investigation and we would not be allowed to touch the house until that was finished, it could take weeks. Ben went on to say that he felt the house would have to be taken down to ground level and re-built only salvaging the base. It was a disaster, it was bad enough that the house had burnt badly and was a blackened centre point for anyone coming to view the properties but, the fact that we could not do anything and had a burnt-out house right in the middle of the development, what sort of advertisement was that?

For the next three weeks, we were under the microscope by the health and safety executive. Not only were they conducting a full investigation on the burnt-out house they were looking at all the practices we undertook. Jonathan, Ben and I had an emergency meeting to discuss what we expected, what we had to do and how long it would take. Most of this fell onto Ben's shoulders as he was the one in charge of the chippy and responsible for the health and safety on site. Ben stated that it could have been worse; had the house been completed we would have had the additional expense of the loss. Also, we were up to speed with all the required health and safety regulations requirements and it had been in our favour that Ben had reacted by sacking the culprit that had started it. This showed the health and safety that we took safety seriously and they would have expected nothing less. He did tell Ben that had he not done that, they may have looked at prosecuting our company.

Three weeks after our meeting Ben came to see me and said the health and safety, fire brigade and police had completed their investigations and we could continue as needed to sort out the mess. The only suggestion from the health and safety was that Ben hold a safety meeting with all the workforce to highlight their responsibilities. We both felt a great wave of relief. The cost of the rebuild was estimated at £46,000; the expensive part was the lost time and damage to our reputation. Ben felt guilty about what had happened and I assured him that I did not see he had anything to feel guilty about. He could not be held responsible for every second everyone was on site, he had to be able to trust his workforce to be responsible and professional about how they conducted themselves. I told

Ben that as far as I was concerned the issue was closed and we would not discuss it again. I offered Ben a drink and asked if he played snooker; he said he had a couple of times. That was good enough for me, I might even win, in we went. I felt that I had improved my game and could put together a break running into double figures. Ben whitewashed me, I only got to the table twice and that was to break. We had a good laugh and both enjoyed the evening.

By the time Ben left it had turned ten o'clock and he had to go home by taxi. He returned the next morning having had one of his sons drive him to collect his car. Ben made it a priority to get the burnt-out house down and rebuilt in rapid time. I spoke to him before I asked Dave to occasionally walk around the site checking on safety issues to ensure no other bad practices were being used and Ben welcomed the additional support.

Dave had returned with the report and expenditure of what the first and second developments had cost to install and maintain the security systems. I thanked Dave and telephoned Mr Green. We arranged that Mr Green would call at the house that afternoon and he arrived at two-thirty. He told me that he had been in security all his adult life and ran a successful company in London. He had heard about the operation we had developed on television a couple of years ago and decided to take a look. He had been impressed with the system and decided that should the opportunity come up, he would try to get involved. When he heard that we were not going to install the same system on the second development, he decided to approach us. I felt that Mr Green appeared to be competent and experienced far in advance of our experience and level of professionalism and that he would enhance what we had started. I made a tentative agreement with Mr Green. We would install the new camera system on development two and he agreed that no price increase would be introduced on development one for five years and there would be no deterioration in standards or quality of service. He also stated that the eight current security guards would continue to be employed with no drop in money or position.

We agreed that Mr Green would cover all the costs of the installation on development two and pay our company £75,000 on top of any cost incurred on completion. In addition, a further £25,000 would be paid in advance and non-returnable as security and down deposit. I told Mr Green I would have our solicitors look over what we had discussed and if they gave it the green light, I would have the paperwork drawn up. We shook hands and he left.

I telephoned both Ben and Jonathan to bring them up to date on what would need to be done to fulfil our part of the bargain. Ben said he had the perfect position for the new security hut. I felt that should this come off, we would have made a little money and provided the communities with a secure future run by a professional operation. It took two weeks for the solicitors to agree on the final format of the sale, having come back to me and Mr Green several times on various issues. In the end, the sale went through and we had the deposit. The next task was for Dave to call a meeting of the security team to update them on the developments that had taken place. Dave arranged this to take place in the security hut on development one so that we had continuity of cover. When Dave came to see me that evening, he informed me that without exception the whole team would have preferred to have stayed employed by us but relented when Dave told them that the expansion originally was not going to be extended into development two and by accepting this sale, they realised that it would secure their future and increase the team significantly.

Ben wasted no time in removing all remnants of the burnt property and proceeded with new vigour. We were coming up to Christmas and the raw materials side had eased a little but was still causing some minor delays. I had asked Ben and Jonathan to extend the Christmas holiday for a further two weeks to allow the stocks to build a little. Most of our major suppliers were supporting us as best they could but, an additional two weeks' break would ensure we would not have to stop or slow down for a good few months to come.

To the disappointment of the family, Julie and I had decided to book a holiday in Spain for the duration of Christmas and had intended to close the house down. Sandra and Martha had decided to have Christmas together and Sandra had a new partner, Bridget. At the last moment, just as we were thinking of going on our holiday, Julie came down with a stinker of a cold and we decided to cancel the holiday. All the family had arranged various events and parties and although they popped in quite regularly and we went to some of the parties it was a very quiet Christmas. On Christmas Day, we were invited to Christmas dinner with Danie and Jake and after dinner, we all went over to Donna's house for the evening. We missed Becky and Jonathan and the little ones as they had gone to Scotland for the new year's festivities. We had a wonderful day and did not return home until very late the next morning.

16

Eight years and still pushing

Due to the delay in the returned start-up, nothing happened until the 14th of January, During the extended shutdown, Dave had arranged for any deliveries to be taken in by security and stored on the secured site. No deliveries happened until the second week of January and then they all came at once. A couple of deliveries had to be taken off by forklift and Dave had been called away, fortunately, I still held my forklift truck licence and unloaded the load. By the time everyone started to return to work on the 18th of January, our stock level was really good. On day one, following the 18th, I decided to go for lunch in the new marquee to see for myself what the food was like. I started with pea soup, followed by shepherd's pie, mashed potato, onion gravy, sprouts and cabbage. And finally, apple pie and custard. I paid my nine pounds fifty and rolled outside, the meal was fantastic value for money and worth every penny. I thanked the cook and the ladies serving and walked outside and started to talk to some of the workers as they came out of the marquee returning to the living quarters.

As I was getting into my car ready to leave, Jonathan pulled up as he had come to see for himself how the canteen was faring. I told him of my experience and asked him to show me around the living accommodation. The flooring had been constructed of a material like tarmac but was very firm and gave good insulation. Each sleeping area had been partitioned off for privacy and the lighting was a little subdued. A double entrance had been erected so that during the night anyone coming in or out would not cause a draught or disturb others. I could not see any form of heating and asked Jonathan how it was heated. He told me that they had used the roofing foam that Leigh used on the roofs in the industrial units and also installed underfloor heating. Hot water was piped from an industrial boiler outside through the piping within the foam material on the floor. I must say I was well impressed. I asked Jonathan who came up with the idea and he said it was a combination of his and Leigh's.

The next morning, I was up and out early walking around phase one looking at the advancement since my last visit several weeks before when we had had the fire. Not surprisingly, within twenty minutes I was joined by Ben who asked if he could help. I told Ben to relax as I had only come to have a nose around to see how things were going. Ben showed me the rest of the development and then took me over phase two. All the ground work had been completed last year and the bases were being poured ready to start building. Ben stated that during the week the first of the road trunking should be arriving; this was the material we used for the pavements I had developed as phase one was now at a stage where it was ready to be installed. Each one of the trunkings was three metres long and came in at 75 kilos; the grids that went on the top weighed in at a further 50 kilos and cost in excess of £300 per unit. The original ones cost a lot more, but as we already had the moulds and the know-how how to manufacture them, the price had come down considerably. The system had been protected by a patent and the company we had used to manufacture the product had received orders from the United States and Denmark.

We ended up at the show home which was not open due to the two ladies that ran it not starting until noon and they finished at six. The style and paperwork relating to the houses we developed in development one were the same as in development two, so we were up and running from the start. We took a short drive over to Millionaire Row where the outer wall had been completed and the gates were in position, although they had not been connected up to the mains. Three of the houses were in various stages of the build and I was pleased to see none of the trees was damaged. The road and pavement in this development were being completed in the traditional way as it would never have the same amount of traffic that the housing estates would receive.

Ben confirmed that we were on schedule with the build on all phases of the development and as of yet we had not suffered any shortages. I returned home knowing that both Ben and Jonathan were doing an excellent job. Phase one was almost complete, phase two was being started, all ground work had been completed and the industrial park was being built; things could not have been any better.

I took a nice steady drive home and when I got to the gates to our home, they were hanging off the walls and a big JCB was sitting on the grass. I drove quickly to the house to find Sandra and Martha sitting in the hallway looking very shocked. They were both ok apart from being frightened and shaken up. I asked where Julie was and they said she had gone into the village just after I had left this morning. I asked what had happened and Martha said she was by the front door when three men walked in with masks on their faces demanding money and seizing anything they could grab. Sandra had already called the police and as she said that, two police cars pulled up outside the house. Apart from being pushed around a bit and having the life frightened out of them, both Sandra and Martha appeared to be ok and said they did not need medical attention. The officers, a sergeant and three officers were being given direction from the sergeant, one was sent up to the JCB and one stayed with Sandra and Martha, while the other one went into the house to check it out. The sergeant started to ask questions of all three of us, trying to get a full picture of what had taken place.

I gave a copy of the CCTV to the sergeant and left him to talk to Sandra and Martha. I then started to make some calls of my own. My first call was to Robert Barnes who explained what had happened and asked if he could come down and review our security. Robert said he would be with us within the hour. I then called Ben and briefly explained what had happened and asked if he could send a bricky down with some materials to rebuild the pillar that held the gate in position. The officer that had gone to check out the gate had taken photographs and when he returned said we could proceed with its repair. He said he would find out where the JCB had come from and I told him that it was one of ours from the site that had been brought back from development two, to re-dig a drainage trench along the outer wall just by the gates as it had become blocked. The work was supposed to be done tomorrow and the JCB would have been left just outside the gates in readiness.

As I was talking to the sergeant and the other officer, Robert turned up. He said hi to both of them and came over to me and asked if anyone was hurt, and what had happened. I updated Robert and explained that the would-be robbers had taken about thirty pounds off Sandra and Martha and a couple of bits and pieces from the house. Ten minutes later one of Ben's sons, Brian turned up in a van loaded with what he needed to rebuild the posts. He asked if it was ok to proceed and was given the green light once he had turned off the electricity to the gates.

After the officers had gone, Ben turned up and asked to see the CCTV. Straight away he said he knew who they were and stated that it was two of the lads we had trouble with a couple of years ago on site and their youngest brother, who must be following in the family's footsteps. They were the ones whose van Ben had crushed. Ben said he would pass on the information to Sergeant Brookhouse. Robert suggested that the security we had was good and the only additional measure would be to put spikes in the drive so that when the gate opened, they automatically lowered and if someone again crashed through the gates, they would stay upright and puncture all the tyres.

Later that evening, I had a call from Robert telling me that the three culprits were in custody and the stolen items had been retrieved. Brian had rebuilt the posts to hang the gates from but said they would have to wait for forty-eight hours to let the cement dry before hanging the gates. What he had done until then was to park the JCB across the drive so no unwanted visitors could enter and I had the key to the JCB. Julie returned home later in the evening and was shocked at the destruction at the main gate. We tried to send home both Sandra and Martha but neither would go stating that they both felt fine and just wanted to get on with things. Up until this point, we had all felt secure in our home but this unnerved us all. If an amateur crew could do this with such ease, what could a bunch of determined professionals do should they choose to and at what cost? Financially it wasn't an issue, but what did concern me were the people at home should it become violent.

Within a week the gates were operational again and the road spikes Robert had suggested were fitted. I must say I was always dubious when crossing them expecting to hear my tyres pop. Life had returned to a steady rhythm again but what had happened always remained in the back of my mind, could something more sinister happen? It's a horrible feeling and I would sympathise with anyone who's had that experience.

The following month, we were due for our monthly board meeting and I had already received the departmental reports from each area. Jonathan did the report for both him and Ben and it read well; raw materials were still proving difficult to obtain and the price had gone up even though we had a guarantee of supply. All the farm work that we had agreed to undertake had been completed. Brendan the difficult farmer we inherited from Denver Hodge had kept his word and paid his dues on time. Jonathan estimated that we were a third of the way through the development and were on target and just a little over budget to complete on the said date, should we have no serious difficulties. Becky said that the club and restaurant were doing very well and quite a number of the workers from the second development were frequent visitors. The snooker hall had proven to be very popular and most nights all the tables were booked out. Donna did not present a report as hers crossed over with Rebecca's report. Danie's report stated that the Dental and Doctor's practices were both proving successful and it was looking good for the new development as this was planned to be a far larger combined practice. I did not give a summary of the meeting as I felt that everyone was pulling their weight and getting on with the job. I simply said well-done to everyone.

As we were in the middle of the year and the weather was good, I announced that I wanted to hold a big party for the workers, suppliers, friends and relatives. I asked Jonathan to get onto the marquee suppliers and arrange to rent two large marquees to be sited on the lawns of the estate. I arranged a fair with all the normal things, dodgems, hook a duck, a big wheel and so many more attractions. I organised caterers to put on a pig roast, a mobile fish and chip van, a burger van and a mobile curry vehicle organised by Talib. I also wanted a small gift bag to be arranged for each child and a nice bottle of wine for the wives or partners of our workforce to take home at the end of the day. I had arranged with the fair people that no ride would be more than a pound as I know how expensive going to the fair normally is, especially if you have two or three children. The date I had selected was August 18th, a Sunday and arranged invitations to be given or posted in this Monday's post.

The event was set for three weeks and to start at one pm. To judge the numbers, we asked everyone to confirm their attendance before the 12th of August and how many would be attending. We knew that not everyone would come, some would decline and still turn up, however, this would be offset by those who wanted to come and at the last moment could not. The response was marvellous with ninety-five per cent accepting the invitation, which made the number upwards of three hundred guests. I had arranged for twenty portaloos, including ten decent washrooms to be set up around the site, and asked St Johns Ambulance Service for attendance in exchange for a donation to cover any unfortunate accidents. We also invited the local police and fire brigade if they wanted to come and they confirmed they were happy to attend but some of them may still be on duty.

I arranged for two free bars to be set up offering quite a good range of choices. The date came and the house was locked up. Both Sandra and Martha had the day off and we were all looking forward to the day. Guests started to arrive around twelve-thirty and by one-thirty the place was packed. The fire brigade turned up in two engines and one crew were dressed ready to depart at a moment's notice. I spoke to Robert and said I did not know we had that many police officers and he confirmed that neither did he. The fair proved very popular with the kids and at only a pound per ride, the queues were quite long. At three pm the hog roast was ready and by the time I got there, it had all gone. Never mind, I was happy with a burger and chips.

We had organised some puppet shows and face painting for the little ones and a petting farm. It was supervised by qualified nursery teachers who were invited, provided they did two hours looking after the little ones, after that their time was their own. I remembered when we went to Jamaica the acrobats somersaulting along the road and had arranged a number of similar acts. People started to leave around six pm, those with little ones and before they left, I made sure that the ladies received their presents and the children a goody bag. I had spent most of the day going around thanking people for coming and the efforts being given during the build programmes. By eight pm, the last of the guests were leaving and the fair people had agreed to clean up the site; by nine-thirty pm the place was quiet and we had our home back. The day had gone off without a hitch, I am quite sure that everyone had a wonderful day and I felt that it was nice to give the community something back. The fair people kept to their word and cleaned the site up afterwards and it was clear that in a couple of days you would not be able to tell the event took place.

Monday morning and the work went on. We had a lot of people telephone to say thank you for a wonderful day, it was nice to know that everyone felt at ease and enjoyed themselves. I had decided to take a trip to the entertainment complex and see for myself what was going on. I walked into the bar area and there were maybe twenty people in, most of them were staff with only two or three at the bar. The staff recognised me from the party yesterday and I was approached by a very smart chap around twenty-five asking if he could help. I explained I was only having a walk around and thanked him for his time. I was just walking into the restaurant, when Talib approached, giving me a big welcome and asking how he could help. I told Talib that it appeared to be very quiet for lunchtime and Talib said that give it fifteen minutes and it would change. I asked how he felt it was going, and he said it had reached maximum capacity on several occasions and the books showed a steady increase month on month.

Talib was right, fifteen minutes later people started to fill the place up and it was nice to see a number of suited people from the architects and planning office from the village here. The snooker club had half its tables being used and it looked like it was a regular thing. As I was leaving, I bumped into Donna and decided to stay and have a coffee. Once we were seated, I asked her about the entertainment room that we had for bookings, she said that they had had two parties and three wedding receptions in the past three weeks and it had paid for itself but not made any great profit. She felt that if we did not have an increase in booking, we may have to re-think its usage. Once the second development was up and running and the number of people was significantly increased, it could have an effect on the bookings. We chatted about the family and Leigh's business and I asked how the little ones were doing. Donna said that Leah was playing up and would not go to school and Billy was just playing up. I sympathised with her problem but could not give any constructive advice.

Two years ago, Julie and I had purchased a small ranch in Spain we called Donbecnie; it covered five acres and housed a five-bedroom bungalow. I asked Julie if she fancied a break where we could get away for a couple of months and relax and enjoy each other's company. The next day we booked our flights and told everyone of our plans. We said we were not expected back for a couple of months but, may stay on a little longer if we chose to. At the end of the day, if they needed us, we were only a phone call away and three hour flight. Julie and I were ready to set off and we were both looking forward to getting away. The past year had been a bit demanding with the restrictions with the developments and we welcomed this window of opportunity and asked Martha, Sandra and Bridget if they would like to come along. They jumped at the chance of some sunshine and we all set off the following morning. When we arrived, we opened up the house and after unpacking, Martha and Bridget went to the local supermarket for a few supplies, returning loaded up and ready to do some serious relaxing.

After we had been there for a fortnight, I had a call from Robert Barnes asking how we were. I explained that we had decided to have a break and asked if he and Kelly would like to join us. Robert jumped at the suggestion and said he and Kelly would be with us in two days. The area we were in was agricultural and I found it very relaxing sitting on the porch just watching the local livestock and hearing the sound being carried on the air throughout the evening. Robert and Kelly arrived as expected around four pm and we had arranged to have an evening meal at the local restaurant. We had a smashing evening and Robert always had a good tale to tell from his days in the force.

After Robert and Kelly had been with us for four days, I

received a phone call from Jonathan saying that Justin had been in touch requesting that he and I attend a meeting in London on the following Monday. I asked the obvious question, why? Jonathan said that he could not get any information from Justin and would only say that he felt it would be of great interest to us. I asked if Jonathan wanted to go on his own as I had full confidence in any decision he needed to make, and he said that Justin stated that both of us needed to attend. Not having a clue what we were letting ourselves in for and not wanting to put Justin in a difficult position by broaching some sort of confidential understanding, I flew back to the UK and had agreed with Julie and Robert to remain on holiday and I would re-join them in a couple of days. I expected to be back on Tuesday and had a return flight already booked.

I reached home around two pm having arranged for Dave to come to the airport to pick me up. He said he was surprised to see me back so soon and thought I looked well and nice and brown. It was not nice leaving Julie in Spain but I knew she loved the sunshine and she was in good company with Robert and Kelly. It was nice to be home and to be met at the door by our three dogs who Dave had been keeping an eye on. I had only brought a small bag with me as we had everything we needed at home and settled down to a nice meal and a cup of tea. Martha, Sandra and Bridget had stayed in Spain with Julie and I felt they deserved the break as much as we did. Danie and Jake had moved into the house while we were away at our request and it was nice to have company.

While we were in Spain, I had only spoken to Sandra's partner twice and this gave me the opportunity to get to know her better. I also asked Martha how her son was doing and she told me that he and his wife had been involved in a car accident in Australia and were at home convalescing. I told Martha that she should take the opportunity to go and see them both with the grandchildren while we were all away. Martha said that she had been saving for a while and she had enough saved to get the flights and that if I did not mind, she would like to go for a month.

The next morning, Jonathan picked me up at eight am and we drove in his car to London. On the way, I booked a return flight to Australia, business class leaving on Thursday and had the tickets delivered to the house in Spain. I would have loved to have seen the look on Martha's face. Jonathan and I had decided to book a hotel overnight and I had booked my return trip to Spain for late on Tuesday. Justin's car picked us up as before just outside the hotel and we arrived at the appointed time at a large, grey building on the front door a plaque saying Department of Environment and Housing. We went inside and told the people at the reception who we were and that we were expected by Mr Harper. We were asked to take a seat while they spoke on the phone. Two minutes later we were escorted to a large board room. On entering the room, it was empty and the young lady who escorted us told us to help ourselves to tea or coffee and left the room.

After about five minutes Justin walked in saying how very sorry he was for the cloak-and-dagger approach and told us that they had a project they wished to discuss that was ready to go; it was enormous and they wanted our input. We had a little chit-chat and then the room started to fill up with people, after several minutes the room was full to capacity and Justin stood to start the meeting. He introduced the people present, from my left, we had the Environment Minister, next the Home Secretary, Green

Minister, Energy Minister, Justin as Housing Minister, Development Minister, Minister for Energy and several others and their aids. And finally, Justin introduced Jonathan and me as the people who engineered and installed the first road system that would be used in the new development.

Justin then went over to a large table that had been brought in and covered by a sheet. He removed the sheet and explained that it was a model of the new town they were considering building. It would be called Cleanwick, and be sited in Devon and at the moment the location was withheld. The town would consist of five thousand houses occupied by twenty-five thousand people creating jobs for two thousand workers during its development and would be the most environmentally clean town in the world. It would not be connected to the national grid as it would be powered by wind turbines and each house's roof would be covered in solar panels. The houses themselves would be the most thermally insulated ever built and the roads would be the most economic and user-friendly in existence.

On one side of town, all waste and sewage produce would be treated by the town's recycling centre. On the opposite side, was a shopping area, including supermarkets, entertainment facilities and single shops. The only vehicles permitted into the town would be electric and for those that did not have electric vehicles, a car-park situated on the outskirts providing a pick-up and drop-off service was available. The town would be the first town ever built in the world to be specifically built to be environmentally green and energy self-sufficient. Justin offered the meeting open for questions and most were asked by those that did not have government titles. The first question was if the recycling plant was on the outside of the town, how would the town cope with the smell from the waste? The Environment Minister stated that the system to be used would be a closed unit and once the waste had been collected and deposited at the site, it would not see the light of day again until it was fertiliser or in the case of hard waste, it would be burnt to supply fuel for electricity. As an extra positive, the excess electric energy produced would be sent to other towns and cities.

The next question was how did the road structure differ and what were the advantages? Justin asked me to explain how it worked and the advantages it provided and the long-term savings in not having to keep digging up the roads. The next question was how did the ring-and-ride system work? Justin asked the Transport Minister to answer. He stated that taking a leaf from the security system we introduced, each house would pay a monthly payment to cover the costs; if they were not prepared to pay, they would not be allowed to purchase a home, this also went for rentals and re-sells in the future. The mini-buses would run every thirty minutes until ten pm and then on the hour until two am and then again, every two hours until six am. It would take half an hour to complete a round trip. With a smile on his face, he stated that the short walk anyone would have to do from the drop-off point to home would be green-friendly and piloting-free.

The project was expected to take four years to complete and at a cost upwards of three billion pounds. It was quite clear that the Ministers had discussed this in-depth as the answers were ready and waiting. This went on for four hours and eventually when we stopped for a short break and hot drink, I had a moment to ask Justin why Jonathan and I were there. He simply said because we want you to build it and then carried on talking to the chap next to me. I looked at Jonathan and could see what he could see on my face, total surprise and shock. I must say that when we reconvened, I was finding it difficult to concentrate, my mind was all over the place trying to absorb what Justin had just told us. The meeting ended and a crowd bunched around Justin. In a slight gap, he reached through to me and said that a car would pick Jonathan and me up at eight pm.

When we got outside, it was nice to be in the fresh air, the car that had dropped us off was waiting and ready to take us back to the hotel where we booked for another night and I delayed my flight to Spain. I telephoned Julie and asked her to apologise to Robert and Kelly and told her we would be back as soon as possible. We had just enough time to wash and change before the car was due to pick us up. We had no idea what Justin had planned, so had dressed smartly but casually. When we got in the car, Justin was already in the back and welcomed us. He said that he was sorry it had all been a little on a need-to-know basis but, that was just how it had worked out. The Prime Minister wanted to have the project up and started prior to announcing it in the Commons and he was holding it back to announce it just before the next General Election in two years.

Justin said we were going to the club we had visited the last time we visited London as it was short notice and he had only been told by the PM to get things moving on Saturday. We arrived at the club and were escorted to a table at the back as it was a little quieter and we would have the opportunity to talk through a few things. Once we were sitting and some drinks had been delivered, Justin turned around from looking at the stage and said he was sorry for the short notice and the surprise but he had had little choice. I asked why we had been selected to build the town and he said it was because of what we had done with the first estate we had developed and what we were doing on the second. I said that I thanked him for putting us forward but, I understood with all his government contracts, they had to go out for general tender before being placed with any one company. Justin simply said it had been sorted and we had won due to our experience and practical approach to solving the problems we had faced during the developments we had constructed. I recognised the look for us not to ask too many questions but it left me feeling uneasy about what may come in the future. I knew that one of the issues in our favour was the pavement system we had developed with a plastics and fabrications company almost eight years ago, the method had caught on in several companies and we had patented the method and idea, what was not common knowledge, was that we had patented it and not the company that manufactured it and they paid my company to use the method and a percentage of profit.

Following our meeting three years ago, the PM who had since changed had been really excited and determined to use what she had seen. Justin told us that she had wanted to see the estate for herself and had been driven up not long after our meeting and had had a good look around. During the visit, Boris Johnson had accompanied her and also loved all they had seen including the security and layout of the estate. I said to Justin that I was surprised we had not found out about his visit, and Justin said it had all been done on the quiet for security reasons. I asked Justin what our responsibilities would be on the build, he said we would have autonomy as far as the build went, provided we followed the guidance and worked with the various ministers. The ministers would be responsible for the spec on the solar panelling, waste site, transport hub and the type of thermal insulation used in the houses. Apart from that, the rest would be up to us. We would use our own contractors and employees and suppliers of materials. I asked how the finances would be calculated, Justin stated that the insulation and roofing we would purchase from the minister's preferred suppliers and the waste disposal, the transport for the hub would be organised by the Transport and Environmental ministers respectively but, the basic sites we would build within our specification using the inspiration and innovation shown in our previous work.

Justin said that we would be having meetings with the Environment and Transport ministers over the next few months and discussing supply, cost and delivery as well as how they would see the project developing. Both Jonathan and I had hundreds of questions but, realised this was not the place or time, all would become clear eventually. We enjoyed the entertainment provided by the show but could not relax with the new extraordinary briefing we had received earlier today. As we were getting ready to leave, I had one question that I needed to have answered today so that I could start getting my head around the enormity of the scheme; when was the proposed start date? Justin said in the next twelve months. We said our goodbyes to Justin outside the hotel and as we entered, I said to Jonathan we would talk tomorrow. My flight back to Spain was on an open ticket and the latest flight out tonight was eleven fifty-seven and I had to book the next flight before breakfast. I met Jonathan in the dining hall and we ordered our breakfast. I think we were both still a little shocked at the turn of events and I broke the conversation by saying that as the project was not due to start until next year and then the ground works would take some time, we needed to wind up the second development as soon as possible.

I asked Jonathan to talk to Ben and ask him to speed up

the development as best he could and take on whatever labour he needed to do so. This would have been a little difficult to ask without explaining why when the build was on target or possibly in advance. Jonathan had told me that he had been looking at a twenty-two-acre site and we could use this as the excuse. Neither of us liked deceiving Ben but we were under orders not to disclose what we had discussed with anyone outside the meeting. I also told Jonathan that if the site he had seen was viable, buy it, as it would benefit us at a later date. Jonathan also stated that he would use the same excuses to start ordering raw materials in readiness as we did not want to get caught out and if it didn't happen, we could use them on our next project.

After a light breakfast, Jonathan returned home and I used the facilities at the hotel to try to relax awaiting my flight back to Spain. On my return and explaining what had happened to Julie, we enjoyed the rest of the break and booked our flight back to the UK. Robert and Kelly had stayed with us and returned when we did along with Sandra and Bridget. I asked what the reaction was from Martha when she received the ticket to Australia. And Julie said she just sat down and cried. They all rallied around and got her on the flight on time and wished her a wonderful holiday. As our flight landed, we got the train to the nearest train station that I had arranged for Dave to pick us up from. We got home around ten-thirty feeling drained from the journey and just wanted to go the bed.

The next morning, I telephoned Jonathan and Ben and asked them to come to my office to get an update. While I was waiting, I called the girls to see if everything was ok. Having discovered no problems, I settled down to watch television and relax. Both Jonathan and Ben arrived together at ten am and we all went into the study. I explained to Ben that we were looking at a new development and that we needed to bring to a head the one we were currently working on as fast as possible. The current development was not due to finish until the year 2018/2019, Ben said the best he could do was shave a few months off the schedule if all went well and they had no delays. I told Ben to use whatever resources he needed to gain the extra time. I could see that Ben could smell a rat and we both felt terrible that we were deceiving him. I told Jonathan to make sure that Ben had everything he needed and full support when required. I asked Ben and Jonathan if they would stay for lunch and they both accepted the offer while we were waiting for lunch to be served with Julie and Bridget doing the cooking, we had a couple of games of snooker, and I was really getting concerned my game wasn't getting any better, thrashed is the polite explanation.

While playing Ben, he gave us an update on the current situation in the development and we discussed the industrial site and phase four. Ben explained that Millionaire Row had exceeded all expectations and would be complete by the end of the year as we were over halfway through the build.

17

Millionaire Row

I felt elated that what I considered one of the biggest stages was well under construction and that I would be able to sit back a little and pass the reins to the family; well, that was the plan until our visit to London for the second time. We were still maybe six months off, but I could see the end in sight and we were now in late 2018, all but one house in stage three had not been sold, all of the stages one and two were gone and two hundred and thirty of stage four had been sold off plan. The industrial units were complete and the final layer of the road surface was about to the laid. The new mall was well under construction and would be completed on time. We were getting a lot of people coming from London to purchase their homes to avoid the London costs. Ben had kept on top of the ground work teams and had them move as soon as possible onto the next stage and this had now been completed for some time.

On this site, planning permission had been granted for thirty properties. I had planned to do this in two halves. It was estimated it would take eighteen months to complete once the ground works were out of the way. The site had some wonderful trees that were well over one hundred years old, each had preservation orders on them and everyone had been given strict instructions not to scrape, knock down or interfere with them under any circumstances. The consequences were staggering, financial fines, imprisonment or both. I was happy to have the trees on the site and felt it would enhance the ambience once the site was complete. As the brickies were very good at what they did and had made a beautiful job of the wall adding some quite outstanding craftsmanship when building, I knew that the balancing act of having one-half of the site looking complete while the other half was under construction would have to be carefully managed as people paying millions of pounds for a new house would not want to be living on a building site. It had been discussed at previous board meetings that it was felt that the best solution would to be concentrate on one half and when it was near completion, separate the two halves with eight-foot-high fencing.

We had been suffering a little with the shortage of raw materials for a period but, due to Ben's forethought, he had arranged quite large stocks of most materials available. We had the first fifteen houses completed by the end of last year and on target or better still in advance of our target. The initial roads were complete apart from the top layer of tarmac and should the plans come to fruition the second phase should be completed by the latest early 2019. Entrance to the gated estate was governed by a similar system we had installed at the industrial site; each family would be given their own unique identification code. This would also register at the security hut and be confirmed by the security guard. All homeowners were asked to report to the security hut should they be going away for a few days so an extra good eye could be kept on their property.

The houses that were erected and awaiting decoration looked fantastic. As you walked through the front door you were faced with a flowing staircase leading to the second level. Although all the bannisters were covered in polythene to protect them from scuffs and the decorators, you could see the beauty straight away. Looking down you noticed marble flooring that had under-floor heating, that ran off into every room on the lower level. As you walked into the living room, the log burner was the centrepiece catching your eye and the bi-fold doors leading to the rear garden. Coming back out into the main entrance area and walking directly across you had a choice of two doors, one went into a cinema room and the other, an empty room intended as a games room. Off this room was a door leading into triple garages larger than most each measuring ten feet by twenty feet with electric doors leading out to landscaped gardens. Walking back into the main entrance area you would see a further five rooms. The next room was the kitchen, and in this house, it had been fitted out as this was going to be the show home. When the other houses were sold, the purchaser would be given a multi-choice of bespoke styles with gold-plated taps, granite work surfaces, fully fitted white goods and different styles of bifold doors leading to the gardens.

Off the kitchen to the right was a room intended as the dining room flowing into the living room and a second sitting room. A second door off this room led out into the entrance area where another door turning to the left led into a large room intended as the office/study. Next to its entrance, the final door opened into what was considered a playroom. Walking up the central staircase onto the landing, you were faced with a floating landing with seven doors off. When standing on the upper landing you could look down from any point into the entrance area. The first three rooms were all double bedrooms with ensuite, walk-in showers, gold plated taps, a deep luxurious free-standing bath and fitted wardrobes. The fourth room was the large family bathroom set in the same style and standard with both toilet and bidet. The next room was considered the master bedroom; this measured eighteen feet square with four double fitted wardrobes, a large window with a view of the front entrance, a walk-in dressing room, again, fitted out with a further three double wardrobes and then into the ensuite. Again, gold plated taps, large walk-in shower, toilet, bidet and large double bath. Walking back out onto the landing to your left a further two double bedrooms with ensuite set in the same style as the rest.

It had been planned that all but two of these houses would have six double bedrooms and the remaining two, eight double bedrooms. Any would-be purchaser would have a wide range of styles of marble, granite, style of taps, bathroom fittings, styles of wardrobes etc, these houses were costed in excess of three million pounds each and people would expect the very best with this price tag. Each house stood in a plot of half an acre with the back of the house facing south to gain the maximum advantage of the summer sun. Each house on the periphery of its plot was surrounded with Euro-style fencing and the option to purchase double electric gates should they feel the need.

It was at this stage I wanted the girls to meet me at the new development. I made the phone calls and asked them to come down. An hour later all three girls and Julie were wanting to know what was happening. I asked them to accompany me around what would be the show home and explained that when sold to the purchaser they would have multi choices of colours, fittings etc of the items included. I told the girls that although only fifteen of the houses had been completed, I wanted them to look at the plans for the estate and pick their own home for the price of one pound each. Donna chose one of the eight-bedroomed houses that would be built in the second phase and were happy to wait until it would be ready. Becky chose the second house that had been already built and was ready to move in, while Danie could not make up her mind between three houses off plan. I told Danie to talk it over with Jake and let me know as soon as possible as I wanted to offer someone else the opportunity to pick a house.

I asked Ben and Jill and Dave and Alison to come down and see me at the development, they joined Julie and me half an hour later, Ben carrying a bag of tools expecting to be asked to do one job or the other. I told them that they had been instrumental in the development from the start and I felt it right for their loyalties to be recognised. I could not thank them enough for their contribution over the past eight years and all the hard work and as well as Jill's and Alison's patience while Ben and Dave were working all those hours. I felt that these attributes needed to be rewarded. I then asked Ben and Jill and Dave and Alison to pick a house each again for one pound. All four looked at me in utter shock. I pointed at the plans and said to Ben, have you forgotten how to read the plans? Pick! They pondered for over an hour while I had another walk around the house; I told them the girls had picked this plot or that and included the ones sold off plan and said the option of the rest was up for grabs. Ben and Jill chose a house in a beautiful setting in the far corner of the development and Dave and Alison picked a house that would be in the second phase. I asked both Ben and Dave for a pound and told them the houses were theirs and that would they all join Julie and me and the girls at our house that evening to celebrate. It was an end to a wonderful day and I felt elated that I had been able to pass on some of our good fortunes to the most important people in our lives.

This development should all be completed by the middle of next year and I think we were all looking at things slowing down a little, without knowing anything about the new proposed plan. Martha had gone out of her way to cook a superb meal fit for any royalty and had stayed over to serve it up. Ben, Dave, Alison and Jill turned up at seven pm and we all went straight in for dinner. I had arranged for the grandchildren, Eve, Alexa, and Nina to come down to help Martha serve the meal and clear the crockery away so that Martha could get off home in the taxi that arrived at eight pm. Eve, Alexa and Nina were going to stay overnight and once they had tidied up, joined us in the sitting room after dinner. In the end, everyone stayed overnight and it was gone three am before we all piled off to bed. As evenings go, it was one of the most enjoyable I had for a very long time. I felt we had returned something to the people that deserved it most and had been a major part of our lives for the past twelve years. The three grandchildren did a marvellous job of tidying up and putting everything away, and when Martha returned the next morning, she had plenty of time to have coffee and a sit down before she started breakfast.

Everyone started to trickle away after breakfast and by noon only Julie and I were left in the house. It was a pleasant Sunday afternoon and I asked Martha if she would like to go home or stay and relax around the house. She chose to stay as she felt as at home here as she did at her own home and should the hour get late, we had a room that both Sandra and Martha used to stay over when they wanted to. If it was late, I would never allow them to return home on foot or cycle and insisted they return home by taxi.

The next morning, I telephoned Jonathan and told him that I was going to concentrate on our new project and would leave him to concentrate on our current build. I said I would be around should he need my opinion on anything but, I felt quite confident that Jonathan and Ben could handle anything that came up. I made a call to Justin and left a message for him to call me when it was convenient. In the meantime, I had little to do but wait. At the back of the house, we had a fifty-metre lawn and then it ran into woodland for about a mile. I had been watching a programme on television about a chap that had a small area of land that he used as a natural area for flowers with a small pond. I decided to ask Ben to drop a small digger down so I could excavate a pond; I knew the ground was always damp, so felt it would hold water naturally. The following day the digger arrived and I asked William our gardener to assist me. We dug out a pond no more than two metres deep and about twenty-five metres in a roundish type shape. William suggested lining it with liner as although it was damp here most of the year, during long periods of summer it tended to dry out. This we did and filled it with water after edging the sides with rocks. William knew his stuff when it came to what type of plants we needed to aerate the water. We then spread wildflower seeds around. Job done, all we had to do was wait to see our results.

I received a return call from Justin that evening and we had a brief chat about the project. I asked if he and the family would like to come and spend the weekend with us and he and I could discuss it further. Justin said he had a rather full diary but would sort something out for the following weekend. Ben popped in to tell me that he had speeded up the operation as best he could by employing a further twenty workers for the site starting Monday and he felt it would reduce the development's build time by the six months he felt he could do. He also said that the industrial site would be complete in around three weeks. I asked Ben if he was up for another challenge should it arise. He said that he was looking at the possibility of handing over the reins of the company to his son at the end of this development as he and his good lady wanted to enjoy some time together. I understood what Ben was saying and told him I would support any decision he may make and I said I felt like I was already missing him. Ben said that they had not made any firm decisions as of yet, it was just a thought they had discussed a couple of times.

After Ben left, I sat in my office and pondered our conversation. He had been the backbone of our operation since day one and he would be a hard act for anyone to follow. I knew that both of Ben's sons were very capable and had come on a long way with the experience gained over the past few years, but they were not Ben. Well, at that moment there was nothing I could do about it as that was a decision for Ben and his good lady to make and I would not interfere with it. We would cross that bridge when the time came.

18

Justin's visit

Justin and the family arrived late on Friday afternoon and we showed them to their rooms and settled in the living room for the remainder of the afternoon while waiting for our evening dinner. Justin looked tired and he said that he had been working nonstop for several weeks without a break and had been looking forward to this weekend. Sally told us that she felt Justin was burning himself out and welcomed the break away from what he was working on. Justin had planned to stay until late on Monday and I told him that we would not discuss anything until Monday and he should just relax and enjoy the weekend. He agreed just as Martha shouted to us for dinner. The children went to bed around ten pm and we settled down with a nice bottle of wine and good conversation.

On Saturday night I arranged to go to Talib's restaurant for our evening meal and after a wonderful welcome and meal returned home and again settled down for the evening. I could see the weight and pressure evaporating from Justin and Sally agreed he was looking a lot better and relaxed. Sunday, we stayed at home and played Monopoly with the kids and Justin and I had a few games of snooker. I was not improving much but at least I won one game.

Monday came all too quickly and we decided to go for a nice walk around the estate. I showed everyone my new pond and explained what we had done and the benefits to the local wildlife. Sally asked if it was a security issue with having no fence or anything protecting the rear of the property after what happened before. I said that the forest to the rear was quite difficult to access from the roads and we had installed sensors between us and the forest that should anyone come through that way they would sound a warning to the house giving us time to investigate. We went into the woods that had been established over two hundred years ago and was a natural retreat for wildlife. Although there were only a few public rights of way we found one at the far end of the wood that looked like it went on forever. After several miles, we decided to backtrack and return the way we had come. By the time we reached home, it was gone five pm and starting the first signs of darkness.

Justin had decided that he and Sally would leave shortly after dinner as he had to be in London first thing in the morning. He and I retreated to my study while Sally and Julie and the children went into the sitting room to watch television. I asked Justin to give me the rundown on what I could expect and the timing scale around the entire project. He told me that our first meeting in London, when we met the Prime Minister, had started a sequence of events that tumbled into the plan that had been proposed last week and although we had had a change of Prime Minister, the long-term goals had not altered. That was why the PM had insisted on my company constructing the site using the best technology and knowledge we had to date. He had been inspired by what we had done, as had David Cameron when he was PM and wanted this to be his legacy and hopefully the start of more to come, including the possibility of transforming large swathes of land currently redundant with futuristic development.

Justin explained that the site chosen was five miles from Lynmouth in Devon and would benefit from the strong winds and open space currently under-utilised but close enough for direct routes to London and other towns and cities. Justin said that I should have had a set of drawings delivered here this morning showing the accepted plans and layout of the site. I went out into the kitchen to see if Martha had received anything by post and found the kitchen empty. I then went into the sitting room to find everyone watching television and chatting. I asked Martha the question and she said that a rolled-up parcel had arrived while we were out for our walk and it was on top of the filing cabinet in my study. I went back into the study and sure enough, there it was. I passed it to Justin and he unpacked it and laid the plans out on top of my desk. The plans were extensive and detailed showing everything we had discussed at the meeting with a note attached listing everyone who was involved in the project including names, telephone numbers, names of their companies and their actual involvement and responsibilities.

Justin told me that as the main crux of the project would fall on my area of responsibility, I would be granted as much support and assistance as possible. He went into some depth as to the financial expenditure and to cut it short, we would be granted government funding for materials, we would buy in from designated suppliers, items such as insulation, and solar panels but the rest we would source ourselves as we would with labour. We would initially pay for materials and labour and on a monthly basis, claim back the expenses. I asked how we as a company were supposed to make a profit. He said that once each phase was completed and the houses sold, we as a company would, after the expense was deducted, be awarded equal shares with the government of fifty per cent profit from each house, estimated at £50,000 per house, a total of £1.2 billion, equating to £600,000,000 each. The recycling plant and transport hub would be costed separately and a flat rate paid to our company separately. The shopping centres, shops, entertainment centres, clubs etc, would be sold in the traditional way and again the profit divided equally.

I asked what the expected start date was and he said towards the end of this year. I explained that the ground works would take three to six months to get enough ahead of us for us to start to build and that as this was such a large project, with so many people and departments involved, I felt that I had to have it checked out thoroughly by our legal people and others within my organisation before I accepted the challenge. Justin said that he understood my concerns as a project this large could quite easily see a company of our size and larger go bust. He said he had expected me to say this and had spoken to the PM about his concerns. The PM had said that, should we accept the challenge, the government would underwrite any losses incurred that we had. I asked Justin if that would be in writing as by the time this project was finished, we would probably have a different PM and he confirmed that it would be. I told him that I would be using my own legal company run by a Mr Paul Webb of Webb and Son in the village. Justin said that he knew of the company and that I had used them extensively over the years and with the sensitivity it would be ok to discuss my concerns with Paul on a limited basis.

I knew that Justin was thinking about getting off and as dinner was ready, we went into the dining room and sat down for dinner. Martha had done herself proud again with a three-course meal fit for kings. At eight pm we said goodbye to our guests and thanked them for coming. Sally as always was wonderful to be around and asked if we would visit them in a couple of months. We accepted without hesitation. We loved being in their company and the children were the best behaved I had ever known.

The following day I called our team that covered all our

legal issues and asked if I could pop in for a chat. The arrangement was scheduled for three pm and I arrived just before. Paul was sitting behind his desk and stood as I entered and offered me a chair. He asked if I would like tea or coffee and I settled for coffee. We were chatting about a number of things that Paul's company had dealt with over the past few years when I told him that I had something that I needed to discuss that was confidential, even from his own staff. A look of concern crossed his face as the drinks were brought in. When we had stirred our cups, Paul's concerned look was still present. I explained that what we were about to discuss was government classified and could not leave his office. I explained that I had been approached to look at a project on a mammoth scale and had certain things guaranteed which I needed him to ensure were legally binding, even if we had several changes of government. I did not need to show Paul the plans or update him any further on the details but said I would bring the relevant documents to him as soon as they arrived. I could see that Paul was itching to ask but also knew that his professionalism would prevent him from doing so.

On the way home, I passed by Mandy's and Milly's house. Even before I knocked on the door, it flew open and I was welcomed with outstretched arms, before sitting down and being covered with tea and cakes. I spent two hours chatting about everything and found out that the two lads who had done the alterations to their home were regular visitors and were more like sons to them both. I managed to get away and in the nicest way, felt drained, but loved every moment of time spent with them. I eventually got home at seven pm and Martha had plated me a cooked meal ready for my return.

Once I had received the agreed written document signed

by the PM and confirmed it was binding and could not be broken, with Justin's acceptance I decided to discuss the project with Ben. I asked him to come to my office and when he arrived, we went into the study. He thought he was there to discuss our previous conversation and was shocked when I told him it was nothing to do with it and that was a decision I firmly wanted him to make with his good lady. I first asked Ben to forgive us for not being able to describe what we were planning and explained to him the reason and asked him to keep what we were going to discuss to ourselves for the time being. I went into the basics of the plan and told Ben it was a nine-year project and I wanted to know if he was interested in the challenge. I said that the current development we were working on would not be finished before the new project started and I proposed to leave Brian, his eldest son, in charge of this development and take Ben onto the new project. In time as this development drew to a close, Brian and the rest of the team would be drafted onto the new project. I could see the excitement in Ben's eyes and knew he was interested but, he said he would have to talk it over with her inside before making a firm decision. I said I understood his concerns and again would stand by any decision he made.

Ben and I spent the rest of the afternoon discussing the development and the new project in further detail and he left around five pm. I had asked if he wanted to stay for dinner and he said he had a nice steak and kidney pie waiting for him at home. I went into the kitchen and sat talking to Martha while she finished dinner. She told me all about her holiday to Australia and her son and beautiful baby grand daughter. She showed me photos and was beaming with the joy of seeing them. Julie came in to see what all the laughter was about and was pulled in by Martha showing her the photos for the tenth time. Martha told us that Sandra and her partner Bridget were planning on getting married in July next year and were going to spend their honeymoon in Portugal and were going to ask if she could take a month's holiday all in one go. I said that Julie would talk to Sandra tomorrow.

That evening after dinner, Julie and I decided to ask Sandra if she would like to hold her wedding here at the house and we would arrange to have a marquee on the lawn and Martha could do the catering for the day. The next day after lunch Sandra came up to me and gave me the biggest hug ever. I said I guessed that Julie had talked to her and she had accepted our invitation. Sandra said she would have to talk to Bridget but knew she would be over the moon. Julie came over and said that Bridget and Sandra were inviting about forty guests and I asked if it was acceptable to have our family present. Sandra was thrilled, she felt part of the family and our acceptance of her relationship never being questioned she felt truly bonded with us all and would love to have two of our grandchildren as bridesmaids. I told Sandra to have the rest of the day off and go home and tell Bridget the news before she burst.

Julie under the direction of Bridget and Sandra was going to help organise the wedding and the invitations were sent out. All of the girls and partners accepted straight away as they saw Sandra more as a sister who lived at our home with the amount of time she spent there. It was a lovely closure to the day and we all felt joyous with the forthcoming wedding and all that was happening. We really felt blessed and fortunate that we could give a little something back for all the help and assistance we had received over the past years and the loyalty given to us by the people around us. That night the house was quiet and we slept like logs until the sound of Martha the next morning and the clatter of pans in the kitchen.

When we got up, the sun was shining across the lawn which had the first covering of frost, our indication that winter was coming and the end of another year. I could hear Sandra doing the housework and as I walked out of the bedroom, she hugged me again and said that she and Bridget would love to accept our kind invitation to have the wedding here. I smiled, said good and carried on. My youngest daughter had taken horse riding lessons when she was young and I had driven her every Saturday for two years to get some training and spend a little time together. Since then, she had not ridden a horse and when we bought this house and were having the garages built, she asked if she could stable her own horse here. It ended up that as you went out the front door and turned right, within twenty yards you came to a high wall with an arch through to the walled garden. William kept the garden in excellent condition and supplied the house with an almost all-year-round supply of vegetables and some of its fruit. He had a good-sized greenhouse and this kept us in cucumbers and tomatoes and the waste from the horses was used on the garden and flower beds surrounding the house.

As you went through the archway to the right stood William's shed, to the left of that the garage complex with the offices above and again to the left of the garages, two stable blocks. Between the arch and the garages was about one-hundred metres in depth and one-hundred and fifty metres wide and this was what William used as his walled garden. Danie was the only one of us who had learnt to ride a horse and in turn, she had shown us. Most of the time it would be Danie and Becky taking the horses out for a ride but once in a while I would take both of them out on my own. I only ever went around the perimeter of the estate as it gave me the opportunity to check the fences and give the horses an extra walk.

19

Covid

On Monday the 6th of January, 2019 we were all due to return to work. A couple of the construction workers had decided to move on seeing the end in sight for the development. I cannot say I blame them; they were looking out for themselves and their families and they did not know about the forthcoming plans. I asked Ben not to replace the missing chaps as I was quite prepared to allow things to slow down a little. It was now moving into early February and we were starting to hear about something called COVID-19. Apparently, it had been imported from China and was expected to be the next world pandemic. I guess like everyone else we just had to see where this was going. In the mall, the club was going really well but we kept hearing about possible shutdowns because of the Corona Virus and this was a concern to everyone. The room I had built with a view to renting it out for social events was booked until the end of the year. Donna had taken over the events room and she had hired three staff to cater for any events that were scheduled, arranging seating and tables, conducting waiter service from the bar to the function room and helping serve food when required. In all the mall was becoming a very good investment and employed over thirty staff most from the estate and the remainder from the village. Talib had got the Indian restaurant up and running and it was getting harder to book a table as it was very popular. Out of the eight shops we had built, seven were now rented out and it looked like Boots the chemist was taking on the last shop.

In March the government decided to call a halt to just about everything due to the covid outbreak. To be on the safe side, I decided to halt all development on the sites with very little left to do until further notice. I did not have to furlough many of the staff on the site as they were mostly contractors, self-employed apart from Ben's chaps. Alison went to work sorting out what had to be done. I must say I thought the government scheme was very fair. I offered Martha and Sandra the opportunity to move in for the duration of the pandemic if they wished to do so. Both said that as they lived on their own and did not tend to mix with people much, they would prefer to return home every evening. We were being told to protect the N.H.S and save lives. We were limited to what could stay open and what had to close. The supermarket and pet shop could stay open, but Talib's restaurant and some of the other shops had to close. The dental practice had to dramatically reduce its services, and what remained were under restrictions of forcing queuing at shops, masks to be worn, etc.

It was only for a short time, some five weeks that the appropriate measure had to be taken for construction, and then construction staff were allowed to return to work. Most of the chaps considered the break an extra holiday following Christmas. After being told we could restart the works on the following Monday most of the chaps returned to work and construction continued as before. We were about five men short overall and this did not appear to slow any of the jobs and progress down. We were not expecting the completion of the final stages of construction until later this year due to the delays if all went well. However, I was being advised that this pandemic was not going to go away lightly and the direction it was going to take was anyone's guess. In order to protect Julie and me, I stopped anyone coming to the house with the exception of Martha and

Sandra. I left the option open for them in case they changed their minds should they wish to move in. If I had no option to meet with anyone face to face it was conducted in the offices above the garage wearing masks etc or on site in the open air.

I was sitting in my office when I received a surprise phone call from William Hardcourt. He had been toying with our discussion and after discussing it with Lorette and his sons had decided to approach me to look at selling up. He was offering me first refusal and should I not be interested he would put it on the open market. I told William that I would come over if that was acceptable and see him and Lorretta that very afternoon. I met with William and Lorretta and William and I had a drive around his farm. He had three tenant farmers that had been working the same farms for two generations. Each farm had a four-bedroomed house, one had a barn and the other two had two each. One of the farms was agricultural and the others were livestock, pigs and dairy. William introduced me to the tenants and they in turn walked us around. It was clear that William thought a lot of his tenants and this was reciprocated. I returned to William's house and we discussed the finer points. The hardest part for William and Loretta was the thought of them having to leave their beloved home as they had lived in the same house since they were married forty-nine years ago. I told William that I would look over what I had seen and come back to him quickly.

Travelling back home I called Jonathan and asked if he could meet me at the house. Forty-five minutes later we sat down in my temporary office above the garage and discussed William's proposal. Jonathan had been looking at William's farm from the aerial photos I had taken shortly after the purchase of the house with a view of obtaining it as part of the estate. It was Jonathan that first looked at the Hardcourt's farm and felt it was worth keeping an eye on it. It was this forward-thinking that I saw in Jonathan that I knew he was in the right position. We agreed with my initial thoughts that the estate was worth around three million pounds. The next day I telephoned William and made my offer. I offered £2,750,000 and told William that I would sign an agreement that he and Lorretta could remain in their own home for life at a monthly rent of £300.00 subject to an annual review. I understood their reluctance to move, they had lived there forever and it was a beautifully maintained home set in three acres of land. The house had no strategic concerns to me and as it was a self-contained plot, I had no plans regarding it. Furthermore, should all the tenants sign new agreements with my company, I would guarantee no price increase in rent for twelve months.

William accepted my offer and I told him I would organise a draft proposal and have it couriered over to him. In April the Covid pandemic was forcing us to shut down some of our businesses. Talib had to close the main restaurant and continue with take-away orders only. Others, including the pub, snooker hall and entertainment room remained closed. We kept on as many of the staff as we could and several were put on furlough, again, most considered it an additional holiday. Some of the industrial units had been forced to close and I had told the tenants to pay what they could and any arrears would be sorted out after we come out of lockdown. Fortunately, the government furlough and grant system came into play quite quickly and the lock down at this stage only lasted a few months for most of the companies. We were reopening the pub, club and restaurant but had to put all sorts of measures in place to protect the public.

William accepted my proposal and contracts were signed with the three tenants and William. He and Loretta were over the moon that I had agreed that they could remain in their home and could not thank me enough. The marquee we had set up for the builders gave as all concerns with the new regulations and recommendations coming from the government about spacing and other issues. We were being told that the virus was spread in the air and we did not know how to overcome the problem of the men and women living in close proximity. Jonathan came up with the idea of installing industrial venting and partitioning each of the sleeping areas. We asked for guidance from the local governing bodies and NHS advisors. We were told that as soon as the front-line services had been inoculated, we would be given priority. We put sanitisers on every entrance and loads within the marquee. We employed one of the local ladies from the estate to do nothing but go around wiping down work surfaces and filling up the sanitiser bottles. We were open to any further suggestions but most of the builders were happy with what we were doing and after being out in the cold all day just wanted to shower and have a hot meal. A smaller marquee had been erected that had a television and could seat around fifty people but we had been advised to shut it down because of the proximity of everyone together.

Having the marquee was a brilliant idea as it saved time travelling to and from work and kept the expenses down for our workforce. Some of the lads only wanted to return to the marquee to sleep so we allowed overtime providing it was needed and with such a lot going on we were grateful for the extra assistance. By and large, Covid was a pain, but we had managed to continue at a reasonable rate apart from a few weeks shut down at the beginning of 2019. The year had generally been terrible, although construction had continued and because Ben had brought in ample materials it did not have a large impact on us. However, it was like everyone was hibernating, we were having shortages at the shops, and people were not allowed to gather in large groups like parties and funerals. If you wanted to go out, there were no clubs, pubs restaurants, entertainment centres or gyms open, the country was shut down. Even the doctors had stopped seeing patients. Danie was a trained, qualified dental nurse at the bottom of the pay scale when it came to NHS professional workers, she complained that their profession had been overlooked in that they were at the top of the list for possible contagion and bottom of the list for safety equipment. She found it quicker to purchase masks etc from the local shops as she could not get any through their normal suppliers. During this period, she applied for a job as a career advisor and after a couple of days of training, she was on more money than she was being paid as a dental nurse after two years of training and six years in the profession being qualified.

20

New Project Stage one

I had arranged with Jonathan to take Ben to the new site for a look around and a better briefing than I had shown him to date. Ben had agreed that he would give three years to the project and then pass on the task to Brian. Once the second development was complete, Brian and most of the rest of the crew would join us on the new project and that would give Brian two and a half years to get up to date and ready to fill Ben's shoes. I would work with Ben on the new project and Jonathan would remain behind with Brian. Also, Ben's younger son, Tom, would be joining us from the start. Tom was an accomplished electrician and his skills and additional support for Ben were welcomed. I was a little concerned that it left Jonathan and Brian somewhat vulnerable but was assured they felt comfortable with the people they had around them to complete the tasks in hand.

On Monday, Ben and I were looking at the more detailed plans and walking around what would be the site, making tentative decisions on how best to break down the project into sizeable sections. I must say the plans were very detailed and comprehensive; for Ben, it was like reading a book where I had to concentrate on the detail and then double-check what I was looking at. Ben and I spent the day going over as many details as possible and we still only covered half of the task. We were still working with one hand behind our back having to keep the project to ourselves and not being allowed to bring into our confidence some of our contacts, which would have made the job easier. Ben and I stayed in a hotel that evening so that we could get an early start the next morning.

On the second day, it was raining which made the job that more difficult to look at the plans and relate that to the ground. We managed to have what we needed by four pm and decided to go back to the hotel to pick up our belongings and return home. On the way home, I had a call from Paul Webb our solicitor explaining that the documents I had asked him to look over were in good order and the company had excellent protection should anything go wrong, including several changes of government. I dropped Ben off at his place and asked him to come to my house the next morning so we could go through what we had to date. I got home around seven-thirty feeling very tired and had a quick meal, shower and was in bed by ten pm.

Up early the next morning, I was looking through what Ben and I had done when Ben joined me. We discussed several main issues and were about to wind up for the day when Jonathan walked in. I highlighted the basics of what we had discovered and how Ben and I felt it best be broken down into manageably sized sections. Jonathan said that if we were to establish the transport hub first and car park, we could use this as a hard-standing and secure site for raw materials and vehicles. It was an excellent idea and one both Ben and I agreed with.

Ben and Jonathan left around six-thirty after dinner and I decided to give Justin a call to up-date him on our decision and progress. Justin was at home and I apologised for interrupting his down time. He said he didn't have down time and I could call anytime I wished. I thanked him and said that our company had looked through the legal contract and agreed it protected us against any eventualities and would happily accept the task offered within the terms agreed. He was delighted and said we would make the

Prime Minister very happy. I explained Ben's and my initial findings regarding the site and how we proposed to move forward. I also told Justin that once the ground crews started to develop the site, the secrecy would be gone. Justin said he understood that we would hold onto it for as long as possible. By developing the site into manageable sizes, it would be difficult for anyone to understand the magnitude and enormity of the project. I told Ben that if I were to offer the ground work team a two-year contract and only gave them one task at a time, although they may feel a little deceived, I would just have to ask them not to ask too many questions. Justin said he would let the Prime Minister know and the other interested parties and I proposed a start date as soon as possible. Justin agreed and said he would get back to me. I asked him how the family were, chatted for a little longer and then wished him a good evening.

That evening Julie and I had dinner late and we were standing in the kitchen washing up and looking forward to a quiet evening before life got very busy when the alarm sounded telling us someone was entering the grounds from the wooded area at the rear. I went straight to the camera and started to look around; to our relief, it was a small herd of deer; we had seen droppings on several occasions but had never seen the deer before. We spent the next couple of hours just watching them feed on the grass. They moved all around the house and early the next morning, to our surprise were on the grass at the front. By the time Martha arrived, they had disappeared. She came in surprised that we were both up so early and started to busy herself in the kitchen.

Ben called to say that he had been in contact with the ground crew and said they would be free in three weeks, but wanted to have a chat about the two-year contract and what it entailed. I asked Ben to set up a meeting and he said he had one for later that day. Ben had been using one of the offices above the garage as his central point of control and had arranged to meet the two main ground crew bosses there at two pm. He had also put on notice some of our main suppliers of the pavement system, brick manufactures and a number more. I asked him what the response was and he stated that they just accepted it as if we were doing another project close to home.

Ben came to the house around twelve-thirty and the two gentlemen arrived just after lunch. Sandra brought them over to the office complex and once we were settled with coffee and cake we got down to business. Ben introduced them as Oliver and Tony Price the founders and owners of the ground working team. Ben had a good working relationship with both Oliver and Tony as he had worked closely with them during the past two developments. I started the meeting by thanking both gents for coming and explained that we were undertaking a new major project that would entail their services for a period of two years. At this stage, we were not at liberty to divulge the location or further details of the development apart from it being by Lynmouth in Devon, and until it was well underway, the magnitude would not become apparent. I was prepared to guarantee a contract that would last for two years and the costs would be met by my company for that period using the same size crew and if possible, the same people. I explained that they would be given a slice at a time of the development and I would appreciate their not asking too many questions about the next stage until ready to start work on it. I could see on their faces a look of confusion and bewilderment and did my best to alleviate those concerns by saying that other parties were involved that could slow the development down should they start to put their noses in and we wanted as few distractions as possible from outside influences. This they appeared to accept and agreed with subject to the formal contract being drawn up and signed, they would have the crew prepped and ready in three weeks, and I stated I would confirm the start date by the end of tomorrow.

Sandra brought in some fresh coffee and we chatted about the projects we had done together to date. They explained that on the back of the work we had provided them with, their company had expanded to double its size with newer and more reliable machinery. It was quite clear to me that the relationship Ben had with Oliver and Tony was solid with a great deal of respect all around. By the time the meeting was over it had turned six pm and I decided to text Justin rather than breach his evening to let him know that we would be ready to move in three weeks and needed him to confirm our start date. By return, I had a text saying the start date would be the first of next month, twenty-seven days away. The next morning, I telephoned Ben and asked him to start the ball rolling by informing the ground crew and suppliers to start gearing up, and advised Ben to start thinking of labour as our development was still under construction and we could not spare or release any of the contractors from our development for another six months. I then phoned Jonathan and put him in the picture, I was about to ask Jonathan to arrange the sleeping accommodation for the workers when I realised that Jonathan now had the addition of Ben's responsibilities and needed to concentrate on the job in hand not working on another project I could do myself.

I started to make phone calls to the people that supplied us before with the marquees and was met with a really welcoming response. I spoke to the same chap that

Jonathan had spoken to the last time and explained what I wanted. He suggested that I use three marquees, one for the kitchen and dining-room and this would double for other functions such as film shows, and the other two for living accommodation as one on its own over a long period of time would become cramped. He said that he could arrange lighting and flooring and the underground heating we had the last time if we were prepared to supply the water heaters and generators. This was a far safer system than any other available, and the generators would already be on site, so we agreed. I phoned Ben and asked him to pick out a suitable site for the three marquees and then started to make calls for this to be the first act of the ground crew as we needed a firm base for marquees and a secure site.

In the meantime, I arranged the internal requirements, bedding, kitchen and bunks. The ground crew would take a month for the compound area and three months to complete the first part of the project and that gave us sixteen weeks to have everything ready for the required labour. The car park and terminal hub were our priority as we needed this done as soon as possible so we could establish accommodation etc. Labour to build the hub could be done at a later date but we needed the basics down now. I discussed it with Brian before bringing Dave into the project and asked him to concentrate on the area we would be using for storage and to tie up with Ben as to the location we had selected for the accommodation area. I felt the buzz coming back after a long period of inactivity; I felt alive again and was looking forward to getting stuck into this project fully.

I was sitting in the living room with Julie and could see the expression on her face and asked what was up. She said that she knew that I was looking forward to this task and did not want to dampen my excitement but, she said that she thought we were going to have more time together and this being a nine-year project, she felt it may be too much and too demanding. I realised what she was saying and said that I would be heading up the project for about eighteen months to two years and during that time after the first six months the team from the second development would be trickling down to add additional support. When that was complete after a short time, I would hand the reins to Jonathan to lead and I would work in the background. I felt I had allayed her concerns for the time being but knew she would be keeping an eye on me.

Justin had arranged meetings on my behalf with the Environmental, Energy and Transport Ministers which I attended with Ben, who told me he felt very much out of his comfort zone. I leaned over and whispered to him, "so do I." The responsibilities of the Energy Minister were to supply all the names of the suppliers of insulation and solar glass we were to use and a contract had already been signed by all parties as to the price and quality demanded; all we had to do was agree with the suppliers a schedule for delivery and in what quantities we wanted them called off at. To help support us in this, the government would also provide an expert in each field to assist in the technical understanding and implementation throughout the development. Ben stated that as far as the thermal insulation was concerned, we were up to speed on the latest requirements, however, we would need support with the solar installation. The Energy Minister told us that although each house would be separate from the others they would all be connected by cabling through the pavement system we had developed and that would allow surplus energy to be tapped into the main grid for other places. It was estimated that the surplus energy after each house and the entire town had had its requirements, would be sufficient to run an additional five thousand homes. All street lighting posts would be autonomous and be supplied by their own solar panels and storage systems. At this stage, the Transport Minister had little to say apart from the two vehicles used for the round-robin pick-up and drop-off would be solar-powered holding enough power for twenty-four hours without having to plug in or needing a top-up, this should prevent them from having to charge from external sources although it would be available if needed.

We were given all the details we required and left feeling confident in our task at hand. Ben said that it concerned him a little that the assistance we would be getting in the way of technical support from the government, he felt would be a little bit like big brother watching over us. I understood his concern and said that at the end of the day it was their project and they had a right to keep an eye on its development. If we remained on target and did what we did best, they would have no grounds for complaint.

On our way back home, Ben informed me that he had put out the feelers for the staff for the site but he felt he would need Alison's assistance. I told him that I would talk to her and Dave on my return home. Dave was already starting to install fencing and security on the site Ben had selected and was spending four nights a week in hotels overseeing it. Once I had dropped off Ben and driven to our house, I went over to the office to talk to Alison and broached the subject that we were developing a new place. She said she had already grasped that from the calls and comings and goings over the past two weeks. I asked if she had any ideas or suggestions on how we could support Ben with the paperwork, purchasing, contracts, interviews etc that he would be needing to do. Alison said that it was too far to commute daily and that the only solution would be to set up a satellite operation mirroring what we had here. She suggested that she come down at the beginning and get the ball rolling with a personal assistant for Ben and a purchasing clerk. Once these were in place and up to speed, she would control it and oversee it from our current location. Clever Alison, I knew she would meet the challenge and come up with the solution.

She travelled down the next day and started to interview staff for the positions and arrange accommodation for herself. She planned on spending the week conducting what she had to do and setting up suitable offices and a central point for Ben to work from. Alison was a hard task master and demanded the highest quality of work from the people working for her. Once she had completed all the interviews and had people in place and everything up and running, she moved onto interviewing workers for the site; once again she would reduce the numbers down and the final interviews would be for Ben to do. A number of our workers working on development two were from London and we had a few of the team apply for positions from our site as it was just as handy using the A303 to get to south London as it was from where we were currently. At this stage they did not know that it was us that was developing the new site and as our site up north was due to be completed in just over twelve months and the new site expected to last a lot longer, I could not blame them. All these applications were put on hold for now as we would use labour afresh for the first stage and once it was all up and running, we would talk to our people and guarantee them employment on the new project once the current development was complete.

Alison had planned for being on site for one week and

this had ended up being three weeks; she would then travel between home and the new project as she felt necessary. On her and Dave's return, I asked if they would join us on Saturday for a night out with Julie and me as a thank you. Still, due to the covid pandemic, we were limited as to what we could do and ended up at Talib's restaurant. Both Dave and Alison looked tired from the tasks they had been given and I asked if they would accept as a thank you a week's holiday on us at our house in Spain Donbecnie. They looked at each other and Dave said that now was not the time with such a lot going on, however, they would love to accept the offer in six months. We had a lovely meal and Talib was as always on top of everything and joined as towards the end of the evening for a last drink. He told us that the restaurant was not as busy as at pre-pandemic levels, however, the takeaway business was thriving and it was accountable for seventy per cent of the company's turnover. We returned home in Dave's car as he did not really drink at all and they decided to spend the night. It had been ages since we had been able to relax and just talk about the families and things not connected to the business.

Having packed our bags and said our goodbyes to everyone, Ben and I moved down to stay for the next few months in a local hotel. We were itching to get started and see the development grow. The ground crew were established on site using the secure compound as a parking lot and central operating point. Ben had moved out of the hotel and arranged to have a porta cabin also in the compound so he would be available for all eventualities. Security had been set up only at this stage using two guards rotating on twelve-hour shifts. Over the weekend the ground crew would be responsible for security using the security hut we had obtained. The first stage for the ground crew was estimated to take ten weeks and they would work simultaneously on the hub and phase one and Ben and I had briefed Oliver and Tony on the second phase. Raw materials had already started to arrive and Ben and I were both off-loading the vehicles and checking off the contents. For some of the more valuable items when ready we used one of the marquees and within nine weeks all three marquees were complete and we were having to use the second marquee for storage.

Between Alison and Ben, they had recruited almost thirty local staff that were in the main ready to start on the first of May, although several had started work as required on the hub area. Brian had more or less finished with the heavy equipment and had transported it down to the site in readiness for our usage. Due to the enormity of each phase, we could not make any effective security barriers around the periphery of each phase, so we decided to use a simple single wire with warning signs, although Dave had managed to make the hub area secure. The isolation of the site would help, that is until we came to the site one morning to find a group of people protesting about losing green belt land. They had set up on the track road we were using to enter the site and we had to call the police to prevent anyone from getting hurt. They negotiated with the police that they would not leave but would remain at the side of the road to register their complaint and monitor what was going on. They decided to set up a makeshift tent complex and kept to their word and did not interfere with the development.

On the 25th of April, Ben and I started to move materials to where each house would be located in readiness for building. We also had to empty the second marquee and get it ready for the workforce due to start arriving in less than a week. Both Ben and I were working twelve-hour days getting bunks made ready, dividing the marquee into sections, starting the boilers for the hot water system for the canteen and underfloor heating and putting two blankets and pillows on each bed. We had decided that each person would be responsible for supplying their own sleeping bag as we did not want to get into having the responsibility for laundry of sheets etc.

On the 13th of April, the first of the new crew stared to arrive. Ben and I were busy settling them into the accommodation when Justin turned up unexpectantly with two gentlemen, one being the chap who had been responsible for the planning of the site, Graham Hinks, and the other his brother, Phillip Hinks. All three were surprised to see what we had achieved in the short time we had been onsite and both Tony and Philip were very excited to see what they had drawn up being implemented. Justin told me he had telephoned me at home expecting to find me there and was surprised to know that I had come to the site myself to oversee the operation. I told Justin that I was here to lend a hand to Ben and that the benefit of being here myself was to ensure it ran smoothly.

By now it was close to five pm and the canteen was up and running although only having to prepare a few meals and nowhere near working at the capacity it would have to achieve. Ben asked if our guests would like to join us for dinner and we all went into the marquee for something to eat. I explained that once all the workers were on site the canteen would be supplying over three hundred meals a day, breakfast, sandwiches for lunch and a three-course evening meal. The cost to each person was ten pounds for breakfast and evening meal and they had to purchase what they wanted for lunch. We started by having soup, a choice of tomato or chicken followed by either curry or beef stroganoff, or shepherd's pie; for dessert, we had the option of apple pie and custard or mixed fruit with ice cream. Everyone agreed it was great value for money and being this close to London, Tony said he would not be surprised to have a queue working its way down the road.

By six pm all three were heading back to London and Justin phoned me later and told me that they were extremely impressed with the set up and progress to date as was he. The ground workers were ready to move on to phase two and our workers were ready to start doing the footings. Within a week, concrete was being poured and the brickies were starting to perform their role. By the end of the second week, I suggested that Ben and I have the weekend back at home as we had both been working long and hard hours. We had appointed a foreman, Benjamin Taggart, and he would oversee anything that cropped up during our absence.

It was nice to be home with Julie and enjoy some home comforts. I did not realise how tired I was, having been in bed by ten pm, I did not wake until almost noon the next day. Jonathan had dropped by to give an update on developments and in turn, I briefed him on what we were doing and the progress we had made. Bottom line, Jonathan said that all of the team, apart from seven, were going to be moving down and the extra good news was that they had knocked a further three weeks off the timing schedule.

Ben and I went directly to the site and were surprised to see the protesters had gone and the site was busy with people working. While we were travelling down Ben had suggested that I move into the hotel and he took over the portacabin as he felt it more appropriate that I as the owner should not be living on site. I think Ben just wanted me out of his way, but I agreed. The first bricks were starting to be laid and from the off, the amount of insulation used was staggering. I had employed a small camera team to make a documentary about the build and they had almost glued themselves to the first house going up. They had given me an insight into what they had done to date from the drawings to the current phase and I was impressed by the depth of professionalism. Four months into the actual build and the first house was complete along with underfloor heating, triple-glazed windows and solar-panelled roofs. It had not been connected to the waste plant as this had not even been started. It was currently being worked on by the ground crew who were proving to be very efficient; they had almost doubled their equipment and crews and were covering two phases at a time. At this rate they would be complete within the two-year contract I had set and was expecting to have to extend.

Once we had established the hub area as far as we could go, we moved all available staff onto phase one. The team from our development started to trickle down and it was nice to see some familiar faces. Before a single brick had been laid Ben and I had unloaded over one hundred lorries and still the materials kept arriving daily. Now that the crews were starting to arrive the materials would soon start to disappear. By month six we had almost two hundred men working on site including the ground crew and the kitchen and accommodation marquees came into their own. Just on the seven-month mark, Jonathan and Brian arrived and while Brian shared with Ben in the portacabin, Jonathan joined me in the hotel.

Jonathan had just settled in when we had a call from Justin asking me to come to London and update the committee on the progress and give a full presentation. I spoke to the film crew I had engaged and asked if the film to date could be loaded into a disc so I could use it as part of the presentation. I called the accountants we were using and asked that they supply me with an up-to-date account of expenditures and a forecast for the next six months. By the Monday of the following week, I had the information and presentation needed to brief the committee. I had arranged with Justin for our meeting to take place on Thursday at ten am. Sitting in the hotel room I went through the briefing several times making notes and altering the script. I asked Ben to come and hear what I had ready and he helped make several more alterations.

On Friday evening I returned home and asked Jonathan to come and see what he thought; again, several more alterations and it was the best I could manage. I wished that either Ben or Jonathan was travelling and presenting with me, but at the end of the day with the big bucks comes the big responsibility, it was down to me. I wrapped it up for the night and went to watch television for an hour before bed, not that I would get much sleep.

21

Presentation

I travelled down the night before and booked into a local hotel. I must admit I was as nervous as hell and not confident of having to present to a room full of people that were doing this type of thing on a daily basis. I called Justin to let him know that I had arrived and he said a car would pick me up at nine in the morning and bring me to the meeting point. He apologised for not having the forethought to book my accommodation in advance. After not sleeping well that night, I found the car arrived on time and I was taken to my surprise to Downing Street, where I was met by Justin and shown to a room that I had been in the last time and told I had half an hour to set up my presentation. Dead on ten am, the doors opened and people started to fill the room. By five past ten, the room was full and people were standing at the back. The Prime Minister, now Boris Johnson, was sitting in the centre and I had just the smallest amount of comfort seeing a few more familiar faces.

The room was called to order and the attention was directed toward me. I started by thanking everyone for coming and switched on my computer and gave a brief overlay from the concept of attending the meeting at Ten Downing Street to the present date. I then showed the film that the film crew had taken, followed by a financial account of expenditure and forecasted costs for the next six months. I explained that the development had been broken down into sizeable portions of fourteen sections. Before we started, we had to prepare an area where the base camp would be sited and this would eventually become the hub site and car park. Sections one and two, three and four were the first build of five hundred houses on each and phase three and four were the sewage plant and road to the wind farm. Stage five was the shopping mall and entertainment site, stage six, seven eight and nine were more houses, phase ten partial development of the hub, just enough to have it functional; eleven, twelve, thirteen, and fourteen more houses finally back to finish off phase ten.

Once this was done, I offered the meeting open to questions. The first question came from the Housing Minister, Roger Platte, asking about the energy and how it was produced. I explained that the wind turbine installation came under the direct control of the Energy Minister and for in-depth knowledge, I was sure he could give a more technical and detailed understanding. However, for the benefit of today, I gave an overall brief. The wind turbine farm was situated 1.5 kilometres from the west side of the town and our responsibility was to provide the road leading to the farm using the pavement system my company developed to connect it to the sub stations within the perimeter of the town. The ground for the farm had been selected because it was situated in a valley on a five-hundred-metre stretch consisting of all-year-round strong winds rising to a crest, one kilometre from the town. Each turbine would generate enough power to supply approximately 400 homes all year round and there would be twenty turbines. The power would be transferred from the turbine to the sub stations via the trunking developed by my company several years ago. This farm would produce more than enough power on its own, however, in addition to this, each house had a roof completely covered in solar panels and the houses were situated in the majority of cases facing southwest to maximise the sun's resource. In addition, each lamp post was individually a solar-powered post with internal batteries for collection of power that even in the darkest of days would generate sufficient power to illuminate the road surface. The additional power produced from this development would be sufficient to power an additional four thousand homes and would be placed at a price back into the hands of the power companies.

The next question was asked by Thomas Green and I did not get his position; he asked about the trunking system. I explained this was designed to prevent the roads from being dug up and ensure that during frosty days the pavements remained ice-free. Instead of the normal pavement, the pavement was replaced by a unit three metres long, one and a half meters wide and seven hundred millimetres deep, weighing in at fifty kilograms per unit. It was made from a reinforced expanding foam impregnated with a flame-retardant chemical. This worked in that when the material came into contact with excessive heat, the flame-retardant material produced gas; the gas formed a layer over the material preventing air from reaching the foam; no air, no flame, no fire. Each unit was interlocked with the other and a one-hundred-kilo hinged lid was placed on the top to prevent tampering; this needed a crane to lift.

Under normal circumstances, this system would be on each side of the road; one side for power, cabling etc and the other side would be for moist materials, water, sewage and gas etc although gas was not used on this site. The front part was reserved for the collection of surface water and was separated from the main body of the unit. To cross over the road, a smaller unit was installed based on the same principle, divided into two separate sides to allow a crossover from either side.

The next question came from the Home Secretary and

she asked about security. I explained that we were introducing the same system as I had introduced in my previous two developments that had proven to be popular and effective and as I had been requested in my initial brief to do so, this included a monthly fee of twenty pounds per household. I informed the meeting that it was part of the contract to sign up for the security, even if the property was sold on or rented out and this option was made very clear prior to purchase. I explained how the system worked but also explained that the number of security guards was far greater than I had used to date, due to the size of the development; also, I had been in touch with the same companies that ran the system I had introduced previously and they were interested in taking on the contract, but that would be down to the government body that finally took over ownership.

They came thick and fast and were relentless, the next question was again from the Home Secretary, Priti Patel, asking when would I expect the sewerage recycling plant to be up and operational. The hub phase would be completed last in around six to eight months. Were we on budget, were we on schedule? Several times I had to stop and have a drink of water as my throat was as dry as sand paper. By the time the questions started to slow down a little, we were breaking for lunch. I was too wound up to eat and satisfied myself with coffee and a desperate trip to the loo. Lunch only lasted thirty minutes and it was round two. Justin had told me that it was going well and that he felt we were winning some of the sceptics over. I just had time to say I didn't know we had sceptics present before the meeting was called to order.

Round two was as fierce as round one, the questions were coming at me from all directions. I must say I was answering them as best I could and feeling inadequate when the PM stated that the presentation was one of the best he had received and thanked me for the detailed information given. He said he had not expected such an in-depth and detailed briefing. The focus of the meeting was then off me and on the PM and Justin for the next hour or so. By the time everyone was done, it was past five pm and my stomach was rumbling. When everyone left the room, I started to collect the lap-top and my briefing notes when the PM and Justin walked back in. The PM walked up to me and shook my hand and thanked me for all the effort to date and asked that his gratitude be passed onto all those involved in the project. He stated that he was overjoyed with the speed and professionalism demonstrated to date and it justified Justin's faith in suggesting that our company should take the lead; he confirmed that he felt the same and said keep up the excellent work. At that, he turned on his heel and was gone.

The only people in the room were Justin and me and I started to finish collecting my things when he said that the sceptics were hovering, intending to have the project shut down due to the cost and usage of green belt land, having had an ear-bending from the Green party and several activist groups that were present during the meeting. It had never been the intention to have me face the jackals on my own and Justin said he was about to intervene and the PM had stopped him saying I was doing fine on my own. I told Justin that it had not felt like it from where I was! He said the PM was over the moon with the whole presentation and those that were opposed had been won over. He said he would arrange for a car to take me back to the hotel and pick me up again at eight pm.

I was glad to get back to the hotel and asked if a table

was available for a meal. I was shown into the dining room and presented with the menu; it was all very posh and I selected the first thing I recognised, and a rum and coke to boot. My meal arrived and was gone in a flash as I was ravenous and I had just enough time to have a shower and change of clothes before the car arrived with Justin sitting in the back. He explained that there were no shows on at the moment due to the Covid situation and said we could spend the evening in his club and discuss the day's events. Once we were seated and served our drinks, I stared to relax. Justin told me that he could not believe the response from the people that had been complaining about the project, and how their attitudes had changed after my presentation. Justin and the PM were concerned that the project may have to be scaled down due to budget cuts but now felt it would have a green light all the way to completion.

We spent a relaxing evening and I was happy to be in bed at just turned midnight. Justin had dropped me off thanking me for the efforts and said he would be in touch in the next couple of days. The next morning after breakfast, I called a cab to the train station and went back home for a couple of days before returning to the site. On the train, I called both Jonathan and Ben to give them an up-date on how the meeting had gone. I did not mention the sceptics or that funding may have been reduced and part of the project cancelled, which would only bring worry and undermine their confidence in the overall development. Ben told me that while I was in London, a fight had broken out in the canteen and he had been forced to dismiss two chaps and give several more final warnings. The fight had erupted over one of the chaps having smelly feet. The two workers we had lost were from the local employment group and would not have any effect on the schedule and programme.

Brian had taken over the development of the processing plant and they had sorted out his own crew to work directly under him. I liked the idea that Ben was giving Brian responsibility as this would prepare him for when Ben called it a day and it also meant that the project would be moving at a faster rate. I told Ben, Jonathan and Brian that I wanted a meeting at my house on Friday afternoon to re-set some of our goals and establish a slight change in direction. Both Ben and Brian had handed over control to their respective foremen and left the site in plenty of time to be at my house at two pm. I had arranged for Martha to put on a nice meal for them as I knew they would not have time to eat prior to arriving at the meeting.

By three, lunch was over and we had a chat about the changes I wanted to implement. We sat around the kitchen table and I started by saying I was extremely happy to see Brian stepping up to the challenge and I promoted him to site manager under his dad. I said that I wanted both Ben and Brian to work simultaneously on two different phases while Ben kept overall control of the ground work teams directing Tony and Phillip where they needed to be next. I wanted Jonathan to operate mainly on our home estate and expand where he felt justified and if the twenty-two-acre site was an option, he should proceed with its development, as far as planning and then ground work was concerned, and then await Brian's return once the project down south was finished.

I asked Ben for an update on the schedule for the next phase of the project and how in his opinion it was going. He said that the ground crew had completed stages one, two and three and would be on stage four by Monday. Stage one was over half completed and stage two and the treatment plant were well on their way. Stage three had been worked on for six weeks only at this point and it would be well into 2020 before it was complete. He estimated that because both he and Brian were working simultaneously on two projects and had enough labour to cover both sites and provide a certain amount for a third phase managed between them, they knew it would speed things up, reducing the overall schedule by at least several months. Ben said that we could not employ any more staff unless they were local as the accommodation marquee was at its capacity and the kitchen was closely approaching it as well. The ground crew would be complete more or less on the expected date and if Jonathan could get planning permission for the site we had discussed, this would ensure we did not have any penalties if the ground crew finished before the two years as we could offer them the new site to tie them over.

Ben had spoken to both Tony and Phillip separately and they both said if they finished early, they would not invoke any penalties as they were more than grateful for the opportunity they had been given to date. Brian was very quiet and I understood this as he was the new boy to the table; I also knew that he would soon come out of his shell and if he had anything to say or add, he would say it. I told Ben to let Tony and Phillip know that we had another job for them when this one was complete. I finished the meeting by telling Ben and Brian to expect visitors to the site on a fairly regular basis as they could expect a flurry of politicians from all parties and to make sure they complied with all health and safety and covid regulations, and only be granted access by appointment and they must be accompanied at all times by a senior member of the team so that any questions could be answered. I asked Ben if the finances were ready to submit to the committee for the past months and he said he would follow it up on Monday.

Although Ben and Brian were to take equal control of sites, the financial side would stay in Ben's care until he felt that Brian was ready to take further responsibility. Ben said he felt the figure to claim would be around fifty-five million and after the comments I had received from the PM, I felt it would get signed off without any fuss.

I ended the meeting by asking them if they and their partners would join Julie and me at Talib's restaurant at eight tonight for a meal on us to say thank you. Ben was beaming having had Brian promoted to joint site manager with himself, and Jonathan was excited to be given free rein to expand the business and develop his own ideas as well as having, by and large control over the estate. I felt full confidence in the team we had and also knew that the three girls managing large swathes of the estate being supported by Jonathan were a winning combination.

That evening we all had a wonderful time. Brian brought his two young sons, Martin and Luke; and Jonathan and Becky brought Suranne, Nina and Lottie. The atmosphere was relaxed and once again at the end of the evening, I invited Talib to join us for our last drinks. Before everyone left, I told them that the development we were working on would most likely be the building block of future towns and cities to come. It was nice to know that what we had done as a team was valued at the highest level of government and a perfect end to the evening and I had been asked to convey to all here the Prime Minister's thanks and gratitude.

The following Monday, we were all back at work. Stages one and two were complete and the sewage plant construction was well on its way. Stage four, the road to the wind farm, was one of the simpler tasks and would be completed within three months, apart from the top layer of tarmac. We had managed to build up quite a stock of the pavement system and at the rate we were developing the sites, we were still in danger of running out. The process of manufacturing was quite slow as they only had a handful of moulds although they had placed an order for a number more. I decided to give the suppliers a call and update them on our requirements. The phone was answered immediately and I asked to speak to Martin. I informed him of my concern and he said that had had some problems with the moulds and was awaiting the new ones to be delivered and that should be by Friday. I told him we had enough for about two weeks and he would have to gear up production. I asked if he could establish weekend working, and he agreed to look into it. Just as I put the phone down, a call came through and it was Justin telling me that the cat was out of the bag and all and sundry knew about the project. Neither of us was surprised and I asked Justin if he felt it would complicate things to the degree of stopping what we were doing. He said that they had already had a meeting at the highest level and it would be brought to the attention of the Commons tomorrow. I decided to return home that evening and watch the Commons debate on television the next day.

I had a few sleepless nights and had been working long hours and was looking forward to relaxing for the evening and just sitting in the company of Julie. We had not spent much time together since the holiday and I felt I had been neglecting her and had stopped off on the way home in London to buy her a nice necklace and earrings as an apology. She loved the gifts but I am not quite sure I was forgiven for my negligence. We sat down to dinner around six pm and as it was getting late, we asked Martha to join us so she did not have to cook when she got home. While we ate dinner, Martha told us all about her son in Australia and how she had enjoyed the holiday. I asked if she would consider moving out there to be with Josh, and she said she had thought about it and decided against it. She felt that in a couple of years Josh would return to the UK and it would leave her stranded and on her own once again. She told us about her grandchildren and how they had grown since she last saw them and she had spent a lot of time taking them to the park and beach. Josh's wife Helen had made her very welcome and they had got on really well but there had been an undercurrent between Josh and Helen all the time and she was concerned that their marriage was on thin ground, although nothing was said to her. Josh had been promoted twice during the time he had spent out there and ran his own department in finance and had mentioned that it was an international company and he could transfer back to the UK should he choose to if a position became available.

They lived in a four bedroomed house and she had had her own room and most mornings the children had come in to wake her up with a cup of tea. She had been happy to return to the UK but at the same time, she felt torn that she was leaving Josh and the family behind. I asked Martha if Josh and the family would be coming over to the UK anytime soon for a holiday and she said that they would not be returning back to the UK unless it was a return for good and included a move with the company she worked for. Martha had got on very well with Helen and liked her a lot and it would break her heart if they did split up. I could see Martha starting to get a little upset so I changed the conversation and asked how William was doing. She said that he was working very long hours in the garden and it was his pride and joy; only yesterday he had come in with the largest pumpkin she had ever seen. We had pumpkin soup for our starters today and I had to agree, it was delicious.

After dinner, Julie and Martha went into the kitchen to wash up and I went into the living room. Half an hour later they both came in to find me snoring my head off. We sat and watched television for the rest of the evening; Martha stayed over and we all retired at about ten pm.

22

Murder

While we were talking, I received a phone call from Jonathan at home on Tuesday evening telling me that the whole development had come to a standstill. A body had been found in one of the houses that were in a position of having the first fix of electrics when the crew came into work on Monday morning. I asked Jonathan to update me in full on what had happened and he said that the crew had installed the first fix on Friday and Saturday morning and when the crew turned up on Monday, Bart found the body. He had called the police and then he called Ben, and Ben had called Jonathan. Jonathan had decided not to call me expecting it all to have been sorted by now. However, the detective in charge had stopped all work until he said it was ok to return. I asked Jonathan if we had two-hundred men and women standing around with nothing to do, and Jonathan said yes. I called Robert and asked his advice as to how long he felt it would take so that we could return to work. He said it would normally be forty-eight hours unless they found further evidence and had to conduct further searches. He said he would make a couple of calls and if he found out anything he felt might be helpful, he would give me a call.

The next morning, I was on site with Ben and Jonathan watching what was going on, and from what I could see, nothing apart from the odd person coming and going in and out of the house. I walked over to the constable on the front marker tape and asked if I could speak to whoever was in charge. He asked who I was and said he would ask inside. A few moments later a chap walked up to us and introduced himself as Billy Crow, the detective in charge of the investigation. He said that the site would have to remain closed until he had completed his investigation and that may be a few more days. I explained that we had over two-hundred men and women standing around at a cost of over twenty-five thousand pounds a day and I felt it was ludicrous to keep the entire site closed until he had finished his initial investigation. I asked if it was possible to cordon off the house in question and let the workforce return to work, and he said not until he had finished. He returned to the house and I returned to update both Jonathan and Ben who had now been joined by Brian.

While I was updating them a senior officer drove up and got out of his car, he came over to us and introduced himself as Commander Street. He said he had been asked by Robert to see if there was any way of speeding up the release of the site so construction could continue. I thanked him for coming and he walked off towards the tape. The officer on the tape obviously knew who he was and lifted the tape high so he could walk through. As we continued to wait another car pulled up and four men got out and started to walk towards the tape, they showed some identification and the officer raised the tape.

After what seemed hours, the four men left and the Commander came over to me and asked if he could have a word. He said that what he was about to divulge was confidential and should not be shared with the remainder of my staff. The man that had been found dressed like a vagrant was in fact an undercover police officer who had gone missing four days ago. The post-mortem was not due until tomorrow and foul play was suspected and the incident was being classed as suspicious. However, the site would be released tomorrow morning apart from this house that would remain cordoned off for some time to come. I walked back over to talk to the lads and explained that the incident was suspicious and the site would be open from tomorrow morning apart from this house. Jonathan said it would not help with the sales if people knew that a body had been found under these circumstances and fortunately Jonathan had had the good sense to use the labour standing around to keep the press well away. I said that with what had happened, the media would get wind of it and we could expect some poor publicity and would have to have a story ready and all stick with the same one. I asked how Bart was after finding the body and Ben said he had refused to set foot in that house again. I said I understood and once it was finally released, we would have to get another team to finish it off.

I returned home and updated Julie on the events of the day and then went to my study to telephone Robert. I thanked him for his assistance and explained what had happened. He said the detective in charge wanted to keep the site closed until the investigation was complete and that could have been quite some time. It was only when Graham Street informed him that it was a government-funded development and powerful people including several ministers and the Prime Minister were very interested in seeing this devolvement released that the detective saw reason plus, he had been informed that the government was paying the wages bill and it had already cost seventy-five thousand pounds in wages that he would have to sign off on as it would be passed on to central government. I asked Robert what else he knew and he said it was for my ears only and that the officer had been tied to a chair naked, after being abducted and tortured for two days prior to being dumped on my site. They had dressed him before dropping him off to hide his injuries, hoping it would be written off as a tramp committing suicide. His stomach was full of rat poison, hence the blood coming from his eyes, nose and ears and unseen parts of his body. He had been working as part of the drug squad for seven years and had been undercover for two years with a very nasty team and it was these people that were the prime suspects. I asked Robert how his family would cope and Robert said he had been married for a number of years and had two children but, he had been divorced two years ago and his wife had remarried and due to the nature of his work he had little contact with any of them. I thanked Robert for informing me and he said he knew I would keep it to myself and I confirmed I would. I sat in the study for some time thinking how this poor man must have suffered for hours before finally dying in agony and what information the criminal team had managed to extract from him. It was a world I had not come into contact with and was very thankful for that blessing.

23

Commons debate

The debate started at two pm and the Prime Minister rose to address the House. He started by stating that the government had initiated a new development in Devon to build five-thousand homes, shopping complexes, a sewage and recycling plant and a wind turbine plant. The entire project would be the first in the world specifically developed to be self-sufficient in energy and dealing with its own waste. By the time it would be completed, it would produce enough energy to supply additional four-thousand homes with electricity returned to the national grid. At this stage, the PM asked everyone to look at the paper that had already been distributed which gave a breakdown of costs to date and those yet to be met. By the year 2027, the project would be complete, and the government repaid from the cost of the development and be in the black. Clearly, the opposition parties had been given advance notice of today's announcement and had many questions ready to fire. As each question arrived, the PM directed it to the Energy Minister, the Transport minister etc, who were well briefed and clearly excited to be involved. The debate continued for several hours and the questions asked were the same as I had answered only a week ago. It was quite clear the Green party were fully behind it and Labour were on catch-up; Lib-Dems were silent and the Commons was unusually quiet for such an announcement.

The next morning the papers were full of it and I think the conservatives had pulled it off with little or no major issues. Justin called me to ask if I had read what had been said and I told him I had watched it on television. He advised me that the site would be visited by every man and his dog wanting to be brought up to date and shown around. He told me that the PM had attended meetings nonstop with the opposition parties and said that once the project had been described in detail with a full financial explanation, all parties were behind the project. The PM had pulled off a considerable triumph and the kudos was impressive.

I called both Ben and Brian and advised them to set up some sort of guided tour as we did not want people wandering all over the place, as someone would get hurt and every health and safety rule could be broken. In all fairness, we had anticipated that at some stage this would happen and had arranged for the two buses that would run the hub to be used to take people around the various parts of the site. Some parts would be a little bumpy, but at the end of the day, it was a building site. Ben set up guided tours at 11 am and 3 pm Monday to Friday conducted by two of his senior people. We already had flash vests and helmets at the ready and the tour started at what would be the hub and drove through both stages one and two, went up to the sewerage plant and then out onto the new road to the wind farm finally, returning to the hub where our visitors were supplied with tea or coffee. The entire tour would take around forty-five minutes and any additional questions could be asked over tea or coffee.

We were surprised at the number of people who asked to be taken on a tour; within the first week over three hundred had been shown around and the tour was almost full for the second week. Our guests were made up of the media, politicians and property developers. Some of the questions were surprisingly stupid for intelligent people and often the same question would be asked several times on the same tour. Then again, this was a completely new development and new to most of the people attending, People could not understand why the houses on phases one and two were not already occupied until it was explained that until the sewage and waste plant was operational, that would not be possible. Although we had developed the pavement system some time ago, it had not been widely advertised and the concept was new to most politicians and journalists alike. The big question was when will people start to move into the houses? Although the structure of the process plant was well towards completion, it would be another six months before it would be up and ready to run. The concept of the recycling plant was not new technology and had been developed a number of years ago. I attended three of the tours in the first week and always sat at the back so that I could judge if people were satisfied with the experience. At times it was a bumpy ride and I would say from what I had witnessed very successful.

I telephoned Justin to update him on the progress of the development and how the tours were going and asked if they were getting much flak from various parties. He said that it had taken just about everyone by surprise and was being backed by all parties who were trying to get in on the political bandwagon to have their name associated with it. The main ministers who had been involved with the project, including Justin, had been inundated with requests to attend meetings and to do presentations. Justin and the PM had received calls from several countries enquiring about the project and several important people from abroad had attended the tours we had conducted. I did not know that Justin himself had been on one of the buses and he said that the guide had been most professional and had very good in-depth knowledge that he relayed to everyone on the bus. At the end of the tour, Justin said that he had listened to the questions and answers and was deeply impressed, and the coffee was nice.

I told Justin that the buses were doing a fine job and appeared to be robust enough for the uneven ground they had been used for so should not have any issues once they were needed. I explained that the sewerage plant building would be passed over to the Environmental Minister for installation by the end of next week and the road to the wind farm was almost complete, apart from the top layer of tarmac; this would be done at the end of the development. Justin was over the moon for as soon as the sewerage plant was up and running several other issues started to happen; the houses in phases one and two could be occupied, and the buses would start to be used. Out of the one thousand houses completed, over six hundred had been sold and around two hundred of the occupants had electric cars. This highlighted the need for us to develop the car park for non-electric cars and I asked Brian to give it some thought. The current site selected for this purpose we had used for the marquees that were essential for the duration of the rest of the build. Brian told me that he had already discussed this with his dad, and the area next to the marquee site would suffice; they would simply level and hard core the area and it would only take a week to do. As Brian had almost completed the access road to the wind farm, he would start to move some plant over to start the work.

Back at home, the preparations had been going on for Sandra's wedding. A marquee had been erected and Martha had the food in hand using a local catering company so Martha would also be able to enjoy the wedding, it did not stop her from keeping an eye on the caterers. Sandra's family were coming from far and wide and some would be staying overnight at our house. Julie had asked Suranne, Eve, and Alexa our eldest grandchildren to help Martha out with preparing and serving the evening meal the night before. Between the girls, they decorated the marquee and the front of the house with flowers and balloons in white and pink. We were expecting a total of around fifty guests including our family who considered both Sandra and Martha as part of our family. The wedding was to take place on Saturday and the guests started to arrive on Friday. Julie said it was nice to see the look of surprise on the faces of Sandra's family who had not seen the house before. Once again Suranne, Eve and Alexa were on hand to show our guests to their rooms and settle them in. That evening, everyone ate in the main dining room and as always, I was told Martha had excelled herself with a beautiful meal.

I arrived back home around seven pm and could not get over the amount of activity; wherever you looked, more balloons and streamers were being put up, tables and chairs were being taken into the marquee and others onto the lawn. The place looked a picture and our main guest, Sandra had been taken off by her sister for a spa day while the preparations were underway. She would not see the place until the following morning just before the wedding, I must say that Julie and Martha and the girls had done her proud. Martha had put a meal out for me that only needed heating up and I thanked her for doing so. She left around nine pm and returned the next morning by six.

The wedding was due to take place at eleven-thirty and the local parish vicar turned up about an hour before. Julie had set up an area for the ceremony and while the photos were taking place a small army would take the chairs into the marquee for the sit-down meal. Sandra arrived just before the eleven-thirty only five minutes before her intended; the looks on Bridget's and Sandra's faces said it all. When Sandra saw the work and effort that had gone into the preparations it was all she could do not to cry.

The wedding ceremony was short and beautiful and the vows had everyone with a tear in their eye. During the photographs, I was quite happy to remain well in the background but Sandra would not allow it; she dragged me and Julie to the front in just about every picture. Sandra's Dad was a big man and had Sandra's personality, the type of person that would always be the centre of the occasion and ready with a joke; his speech had everyone laughing and added to the wonderful day. Her best woman, her sister, delivered a heartfelt speech with some insight about when Sandra first declared she was gay; it had Sandra cowering as best she could and everyone laughing. Julie and I had never met any of Sandra's family and we warmed to them from the off. Sandra told us that they had struggled for years to make ends meet and lived on overdrafts and loans. They had impeccable manners, and were polite and grateful for what we had done for their daughter. I told her dad that we were honoured to lay this on for Sandra and considered her part of our family as much as he did his own. I told her dad that I didn't want to offend him or belittle him in any way, but we had booked a fortnight's honeymoon in Cyprus for her and asked if he would give it to Sandra and Bridget as if it was from him. I told him that she had been a rock for our family for years and doing what we had done this weekend was our privilege and honour and it would be the perfect end to the day to see her and Bridget leave for their honeymoon.

He considered my proposal and I understood what I felt was going through his mind; after several minutes he shook my hand and said he would love to do it. I thanked him and passed over the tickets. Once the photos were over, we all started to file into the marquee for our meal. The catering staff were excellent and we had the seating arranged so that all the members of Sandra's and Bridget's immediate families were on the top table and the guests were intermingled with our family. Each table had several bottles of wine on them and a bottle of champagne for the toast. By the time the wedding was over, I think everyone was the better for drink. Sandra's dad had given Sandra and Bridget the holiday tickets and the happy couple were preparing to leave. The original plan was that once the wedding was over, the guests would leave. I asked all those that had stayed the night before to be our guests for a second night, there was no way they could have driven home that evening; all accepted our invitation and it allowed us to get to know Sandra and Bridget's families a little better.

The following morning everyone started getting up quite early, some looked like death warmed up suffering from the hangover from hell. Julie had set up in the kitchen and had bacon and sausage baps and sandwiches at the ready, and by noon everyone had left. The last to leave was Sandra's and Bridget's dads. I was in the kitchen helping devour some of the sausage sandwiches when they came in and thanked both Julie and me. It was nice of them to take the trouble to come and see us and say what they had to say; the entire weekend had been really nice and we thanked our guests for coming and were a little sad to see them go, they were such nice people.

On Monday morning we returned to the site, we would be starting on the shopping mall and entertainment centre by the beginning of next month and this was being conducted by Ben while Brian would start on phase six, the third set of five-hundred homes. The ground crew were well in advance of us and were already working on phases thirteen and fourteen; the suppliers of the pavement fabrication had resolved their issues and had started to build stock. I asked Martin to maintain weekend shifts until they had several thousand in stock. Martin said that he had been getting orders from abroad and would be maintaining the weekend shift until the middle of next year. We had been on the project now for over two years and it was going very well; we were ahead of schedule and word coming back from the government was very encouraging.

During my conversation with Justin, he highlighted his surprise at the speed we were getting the job done. I told him that as they had the plans done and dusted that was half the battle. We had been submitting our monthly bills for the cost of materials, labour and fuel to Justin on a regular basis; these had been paid promptly and we had no complaints but I knew that the sooner the houses were occupied, the better. We as a company would not see any profit from the project until it was complete and the last house sold.

While I was talking to Justin, Brian walked in saying that the secure compound had been damaged by activists and it was only by luck that one or more of the marquees had not gone up in flames. I ended the call with Justin and went with Brian to the compound. Graham the chap responsible for issuing the materials out was doing just that when the attack happened. He was starting to take stocks down to phase six and when he returned, the roofing strut had been doused in petrol and set alight. He had managed to get the fire under control with the help of some of the lads, but the damage was considerable. The fire had not spread to the flooring as Graham had the pavement sections stacked between the roofing struts and flooring, otherwise, we could have lost the lot. While Brian had been fetching me, Ben had taken charge and was cleaning up the area to assess the damage. He estimated the cost to be several thousand pounds but would not have any significant effect on our progress. Graham stated that we were due another delivery of struts tomorrow and were lucky in some respects this had happened today and not tomorrow.

I waited for Ben and Brian to finish sorting out what they needed to do and asked if we had any suspects. Ben said we were none the wiser and would need to contact the police and put security on in case of another attack. Up until this incident, we had suffered no theft in any quantity and apart from the protests at the beginning of the project, we had had nothing. We had not put security in place as we were a fair distance from the nearest villages and felt it was not necessary. That all changed with this one act, and when we sat back and looked at the possible implications, with lunch about to be served and some of the workers in the canteen and others in the sleeping quarters getting ready for dinner, we could have had a disaster on our hands. When the police arrived, Brian showed them what we had found out which wasn't much and we asked if they had any advice for us. The officers that attended clearly were taking this seriously and brought in forensic people to see if they could shed any light on the incident. No one had seen anything out of the ordinary and the police said they were trying to find clues without any luck.

While all this was going on, Ben had been arranging additional security to work with the two security guards that would be with us in the morning. Ben had arranged for two current chaps to cover until then. When the security arrived, we were going to have one keep an eye on the secure compound and the other just walk around the site, this would be continued twenty-four hours a day, seven days a week. At the end of the day, the police had no more idea who had caused the fire than we did. We'd had the protesters around a couple of times over the two years and they were our prime suspect but we had no evidence and with the security now on site, we all felt a little better.

By the third week of introducing the buses doing the tour around the site and the development being made public, the numbers had started to reduce and we dropped off one of the buses. In all fairness, everyone was being a little more vigilant and both Ben and Brian told me that anyone coming onto the site was being asked by the workforce to prove why and who they were. The development was flying, Ben had put together groups of people and they worked autonomously from the other groups, each group contained, four brickies, one plumber, one electrician, two plasterers, and two chippies. Once one group had completed their part they moved on to the next build; the system worked well and all the decoration was done by a separate team.

We were now starting to wind the site down for Christmas and Brian had suggested having a party in the marquee for the workers. I asked what he had in mind and Brian said that if we supplied the Christmas meal, the chaps could finish at two pm on the last day and have a nice meal before they started home. I told Brian I would give it some thought. I went to the catering staff and asked what they felt about putting on the Christmas dinner for the two hundred staff and they were all up for it. The plan was that the day before the staff would start to prepare most of the ingredients in readiness for the next day; after breakfast, in the morning the catering team would shut the marquee to prepare the tables and meals. Due to the size of the operation, the people catering for the site had been swamped with the demand and we had to pass it on to a professional catering company. They had taken on our staff and were doing a fantastic job. The catering company had agreed to pay their staff triple time for the day and I had agreed to meet the additional cost. I informed both Brain and Ben that I felt it better to give the team the day off with pay and if any of them decided to go home on the evening before, then that was their decision; as long as they confirmed that was what they wanted to do. Brian said he would pass the word around and come back with the numbers by Thursday. The marquee was set up although a little cramped and the party started at eleven am. Ben, Brian and I helped serve the food to the tables and we supplied beer and wine to each table. Most of the workers were planning on heading home just after the meal and by the end, we only had three men and one woman drunk, they left the next day feeling very hung over. The party was a roaring success. I thanked everyone for the effort they had made during the past two years and wished them a merry Christmas and happy new year and return to the site in January.

We had achieved a great deal over the past two years and the future was looking good. Phases one, two, three and four were complete, phases five and six were well on their way; the ground crew had completed the week before and had agreed to move to the site Jonathan had purchased closer to home. I said my goodbyes to both Brian and Ben and checked off the security guards before leaving. They told me that they had volunteered for the duty as they were both single and would have only been spending Christmas on their own. I felt guilty walking away knowing how their Christmas was going to pan out. By the time I had driven back home, it was almost midnight, apart from one light the house was in darkness. I let myself in and went into the kitchen to make a drink. Rooting around for something quick to eat, I found that Martha had left a shepherd's pie dinner that I only had to heat up. As I was busy getting my dinner ready and doing my drink, Julie walked in and made me jump. She had clearly been asleep and said the beeping of the microwave had woken her up. We both sat and talked for a bit while I ate my dinner and then retired to bed.

The next morning, I woke to find Julie had already gone downstairs and it was past ten o'clock. I joined her in the kitchen and apart from her and me, the house was empty. Over breakfast, she said that the family were all coming later and some were staying overnight while Donna, Leigh and the kids were going on holiday to Spain. Julie had been preparing the Christmas dinner ready for tomorrow and said that Martha, Sandra and Bridget were going to be staying as well. I started to look forward to the forthcoming week. I hadn't had a chance to talk to Sandra and Bridget about their honeymoon and wanted to know all the details. Julie said Jonathan would be calling later to update me on the events over the past few weeks. I poured myself a rum and coke and went into the snooker room to have a knock around.

I did not drink much and was just halfway down the glass when Jonathan walked in. He told me that the twenty-two-acre site he had obtained was ready for the ground crew to start on after Christmas. He had been looking at a neighbour's farm, some seven hundred acres that were up for three million and would be having a closer look next year. It had five tenant farmers, three of whom were long-term tenants and the other two farms kept changing and had changed several times over the past three years. The farming part of our estate was running very well, while the entertainment part of the complex had started to recover and then had gone down again due to the lingering covid crisis. He had spoken to Talib and the takeaway side of the business was booming but, the restaurant was suffering. Donna and Becky said they were in a difficult position facing the same issues. Danie said that the dental and doctor's surgery was doing well financially but still struggling to see patients face to face. The add on as she called them, she had decided not to move forward at the moment and would wait to see how the pandemic went over the next few months.

Jonathan and I discussed the issues in depth and decided that as far as the entertainment side of the business was concerned, we would just have to wait it out and see how things turned out next year. Jonathan said he had been approached by the owner of the wooded area at the rear of our property, covering some 300 acres in a long narrow strip stretching back for about two miles. The owner did not want to sell off the land for some big company to come in and cut down all the trees and had decided to see if we were interested, providing we would maintain it as a wood. I asked if any price had been discussed and Jonathan said it was still in the early stages and they had not discussed it. I told Jonathan that if the price was good, make the deal as it would add to the security of the estate and that I had met one of the protesters down on the Devon complex that told me he had tried to set up an area of woodland to live in and live off the land, it may be something to look into.

I had been playing snooker and just talking to Jonathan when Julie called me for dinner. I asked if Jonathan would join us and we all went into the dining room to eat. I told Jonathan that I had been in discussion with some manufacturers, the ones that did our pavement trunking system and they wanted to expand and go into injection moulding as well. I had been a qualified plastics technician for many years and although I would be behind now on the up-to-date technology the principles would not have changed. I said I would be following this up and would keep him informed as it was an area I knew quite well and was interested in. Jonathan and I continued to discuss matters of the estate over dinner and by the time he left, it was getting dark.

Julie and I were sitting in the living room when the gate alarm went off and announced that Dave and Alison had come for a visit. I buzzed them through and welcomed them at the door. We all went back into the living room and spent the rest of the evening talking and relaxing. Before we realised, it had gone midnight and I suggested that Dave and Alison spend the night. The beds were all made up so they had a choice of where to sleep. The next morning, Dave was up with the larks and I came down around nine. Dave and I went into the snooker room and Alison joined Julie and Martha in the kitchen. Martha wanted to set up the Christmas dinner for everyone and Julie wanted to help. She asked Alison if they would like to join us for dinner and Alison said they were due at Hannah's and Becky was joining them.

Dave and Alison left at about twelve and the family started to arrive around two. Becky and Donna helped serve dinner and Martha and Julie joined us to sit down. Jake and I went into the kitchen to do the washing up and were hit with a huge pile of it. We insisted the girls go into the sitting room while Jake, myself and in the end with a little pressure from the girls, Jonathan joined us and did the washing up. We had stopped doing presents years ago when I won the lotto and only did them for the little ones. Nina and Lottie were straight into tearing off the wrapping paper and it was at this point that Danie and Jake told us she was expecting and the child would be born in June. We were all over the moon. Danie had always been the favourite auntie and had wanted a baby of her own for a long time and now her dream was coming true; to compound our delight, she told us she was expecting twins. This could not be better end-of-the-year news, our tenth and eleventh grandchildren!

The business was going well and we were still expanding. If things continued to go well, I would have loved to have gone back into injection moulding for the trade as well as having our own in-house products. A lot of companies go bust because they rely on other companies supplying them with work; if you have your own product and it is selling fast with a growing and expanding world market and you have the patents, it had to be a winner. Come early January I would be talking to people on this subject to see where it would lead and if it was a viable option for us to take. My knowledge of the industry was quite good and I felt this would hold us in good stead for the future, should we choose to move into this market.

24

New year, new company

January 2021 and we were back in the thick of it. With exception of one lady, all the workforce had returned and were on site working by the 6th of January. Apart from some rain, the weather had been good to us and things had gone well. I had arranged to meet the two chaps that manufactured and did the trials and produced the pavement system we currently used. I discussed with them what options were available to us. They had come up with a plan to move into a double unit each of twenty-five thousand feet and use one unit for the pavement process and the other for injection moulding. They were talking about replacing the moulds for both processes as the old ones were getting tired and were starting to show real signs of wear. The plan they had did not involve my company as they were planning on doing it on their own and financing it through bank loans and overdrafts. I had the patent for the moulds and design for the pavement project but, the injection moulding moulds were nothing to do with me. The product was used as fixtures and fittings within the pavement system and they had designed and developed those.

I knew from keeping an eye on the two of them that although they had made a lot of money from manufacturing the product, they were also spending it as fast as it was coming in. I liked both Billy and John but, they were not good at protecting and advancing their business and I was concerned that if they carried on with their plan and overstretched their finances, they would be open to being bought out or the bank repossessing the business. This I was not prepared to allow to happen, I had too much invested in the pavement system to allow it to be taken over or delay production. Although we had a fair amount of stock due to the seven-day-a-week production, it would only last at best one phase of the development. I made it quite clear that I was not happy with their plan and started to explain why. I informed them that I knew they were over-extended at the bank and they had not been managing the finances of the company well. The moulds they were using should still be in excellent condition and had they been paying attention and been at the factory more they would have seen what was going on, on the shop floor. I accepted they now needed to be replaced as I had seen the standard of the finished product myself on site and that is why I had been looking at what had been going on. I went on by saying I had spoken to some of my contacts and they told me that if they continued this way, the company would go under by the end of the year.

They both looked at me and I could not tell if they were ready to tear my head off or walk out of the meeting. John said it was not his fault and that Billy had been gambling and John had had to bail him out and had used the company as collateral on several occasions. I asked John to give me a ballpark figure on what they owed, he told me that they had covered the debt with the casino and were having to deal with some chaps Billy owed money to over Poker. I asked again what they owed, and Billy said about ninety-seven thousand. The building they operated from was rented and they were in arrears for the past three months; their suppliers were refusing to give any further credit as they owed then another twenty thousand. I asked if they both had a problem with gambling and Billy said it was just himself, and that he had been trying to get out of the problem and it had just got worse as the interest on some of the loans was fifty per cent and they had only been paying off the interest.

I liked both Billy and John and had what I thought was a good working relationship with them; this had taken me by surprise. I knew they were spending money as fast as it was coming in but, I did not know how much trouble they were in. Billy was the planner and manager of the finances and John had been in charge of the manufacturing, they had both been negligent in their duties and it was quite clear that had it been left to continue, it would go belly up. I told Billy that we needed to go through the finance in detail and find out the state of the company and then how much he owed in total. Billy and I sat for the rest of the day going through the books and discussing his debt. The company was in better condition financially than I thought, apart from the suppliers refusing any further credit and demanding twenty grand and a second supplier demanding a further fifteen grand, and the landlord demanding eight thousand; that was the total debt. Billy's problem was bigger than he had stated, when John had gone out of the office to fetch drinks, Billy told me he owed a further fifteen thousand to online gambling and a further five to the bookies. It turned out that Billy owed a total of fifty-five thousand and the company owed twenty-eight plus they had a wage bill coming up they could not pay of another eleven thousand. Between them, they were in a hole for over one hundred thousand and also needed new moulds on all fronts and to top it all, were about to be evicted. I told the lads I would return tomorrow to discuss this further and left the factory.

I telephoned Jonathan and updated him on our discussion and asked if any of the larger units in either of the industrial parks were available. Jonathan said that he had one on the second development available and another about to become available on the first. It was not ideal but it would have to do. I telephoned some of my old contacts in injection moulding to find out if anyone had the spare capacity to make a suit of tools and then rang our current suppliers who manufactured the original set of moulds for the pavement system to see if they could help. They were surprised to hear from me and told me the mould should have lasted for a further fifty thousand shots and thought my call had been to have a duplicate set made to increase production.

The next morning, I turned up at the factory at ten am and went up to the office. John was sitting and talking to the foreman and the conversation did not look good. From what I could understand from the snippets of the little I heard John told the foreman that they may have a problem with paying the wages this month. I could not afford to have the workforce walk out so I interceded and told the foreman that the wages would be met and not to say anything to the rest of his crew and I would come and talk to him later. He looked at me and I guessed about to say who the hell are you when John told him it was ok, and we would speak to him shortly. When the foremen left the office, I asked John where Billy was. He didn't know. He had tried calling him and it went through to voice mail. Billy and John were 50/50 partners in the company and it was pointless talking to only one of them, so I asked John to show me around the factory. We discussed the issue regarding the moulds and it turned out that the problem had accrued due to not having any mould release and the moulds were damaged because of it. The foreman had been watching us walk around and John called him over and introduced me to him explaining I owned the patents of the moulds and was their main customer. I could see for myself the difficulties and damage being caused by removing the product from the moulds and asked John to stop any further production until they had some mould release. John passed on the message to Simon and once the exiting product was out of the mould, work stopped. John said he would send his driver over to pick up some mould release and he could be back in a couple of hours. I gave the driver fifty quid and sent him on his way.

Just as he was leaving, Billy walked in and without stopping to say hi, went up to the offices. John looked embarrassed and I said shall we go up. When we entered the office, Billy was slumped in his chair and looked like he had been drinking. He said hi and asked what was happening. I left it to John to explain what was going on and Billy produced a document from this pocket saying he had been talking to his solicitor and had a signed contract putting John in charge of his shares of the company and that he had also been offered a place in rehab for his drinking and drug problems. This was news to me and I could see by the look on Billy's face that he was uncomfortable with what was accruing. At that Billy got up and walked out. I looked at John and asked if he was ok, he slumped down into the chair and said nothing for quite some time. I sat and waited, giving him some time to compose himself. When John was ready, I started to talk. I told him that the company was beyond putting back on top without a large financial investment, I told him that if he signed over the company to me, I would settle their debts and offer John a position as manager running the shop floor, I would not allow Billy to return under any circumstances until he had been clean and dry for at least twelve months and then we would look and see if we had a position for him. I estimated I would need to invest a minimum of two hundred and fifty thousand to get the company back online. I explained that John would be an employee of my company and I would expect one hundred per cent effort from him to lead his team, anything less and we would have to part ways. John accepted my terms and I told him to get whatever paperwork he needed, and we would go and get a contract drawn up and signed.

I felt for Billy and John but more so for John, they had been a good team and it had ended in disaster and humiliation for both of them. At least Billy had the good sense to get help when he needed it, and in time with a little luck, he might be able to bounce back. I asked John to assemble the workforce and when gathered I explained that I was the new owner and that I would be investing in the company and expected everyone to pull their weight. From what I had seen the chaps were working in difficult conditions with little support and a lack of proper tools to do the job. I did not inform them that I would be moving location in time as I needed them to continue producing until I was ready to move the operation further north. John and I managed to get a contract drawn up and signed the same day and I telephoned the suppliers and paid the arrears. I gave John several cheques made out to various people on John's advice to pay off Billy's debt.

The next day I called the suppliers of the moulds for the pavement design and ordered two complete sets be made up with modifications to the release method. I then called the company that made the injection moulding tools and ordered a new set. I needed four injection moulding machines and some good people to run the factory once it was up and running. When I had been involved years ago the Germans and Japanese were the main suppliers of injection moulding machines, and it was these that I went to in the hope they could supply me without too much delay. Both companies could supply me from stock from within the UK and offered to install them and give whatever training was required as part of the sales price. I telephoned Alison and asked her to find some capable injection moulding technicians and some blow mould technicians as soon as possible. I made several calls to robotic companies and arranged for them to send written quotations for the implementation of robotics on each injection machine once they had received the samples of the moulding. The new plant was about thirty miles from the place I wanted to set up and with this in mind, I decided to talk to the workforce and see if any of them would consider moving to the new site.

I arrived on Thursday morning and John had the chaps ready for our chat; I explained that with the bad blood created with the landlord from not paying the rent we were not able to stay on this site, as the landlord knew or owned most of the rented factories or the other landlords, we had no option other than to move site. John had told me that he had selected his workforce because they were good at what they did and it had taken two years to fine-tune it into the team it was now. This I conveyed to the lads and told them that I was in a position to relocate further north by thirty miles, I would pay a one-off moving expense to assist in the move or could commute daily if they choose to do so. I would not be offering anything extra if they chose the latter option. I explained that I would be investing a large amount of money into the company and as a result, they would have the benefit of working with new tools and equipment and up-to-date technology. The first question was how much of an inducement would they be offered? I said that would depend on their circumstances; if they owned their own home, were married and their wife or partner worked, if they had children at school and other extending circumstances, but the most it would be was five thousand pounds and capped at that. I said that if they owned their own home, I could put them in contact with a company that arranged mortgages and they could advise them as individuals. I understood that this was a major decision they had to make and I asked that they give it some thought over the next few days; I would return on Monday and if they had any questions, I would do my best to answer them. I was asked what the alternative was to moving north. I simply said they would be made redundant within the normal government redundancy system.

John and I returned to the office and Simon followed us in. He asked if he could have a word and John said fine go ahead, Simon had been with John from the beginning and John had told me he had a great deal of respect for Simon's knowledge and experience. Simon said that he wanted to go where the work was and as he was single and had no children, he wanted to know how he would fair in the move and what position he would be offered at the new site. John looked at me and I said that he was a valued member of the team and I would continue and be happy to have him lead it as foreman when the move occurred. As for the financial inducement, with no commitments, it would be fifteen hundred pounds. Simon said thank you and then said, sign me up. I thanked him for coming to see us and told him to confirm his acceptance on Monday.

I turned to John and asked what he would be doing, he said that he needed a job and thirty miles was not far, he would move closer as he had no commitments here and was looking forward to the new challenge. We discussed his salary and agreed that it would start today and I would expect nothing but one hundred per cent from him and for him to organise the move up north from this side. I told him to keep the machines running right up until the last possible moment and organise a sale of all of the injection moulding machines once production had ceased and to bring with him the blow machines. John asked how would we continue to manufacture and I told him to come and see me at home in two weeks.

The next two weeks were frantic, the building we wanted to use needed to be decorated and I had asked Leigh to come in and spray paint the walls and lay a polymer-type floor that was hard-wearing and reflected the light. The building was still quite new and looked fantastic and I decided to set this up as the injection moulding unit. I had asked Jonathan to see if we could persuade any of the tenants in similar-sized buildings to move to the other site, this he had done at a cost of us having to pay for the move and compensate the guy as well but, at the end of the day, it would be worth it. Leigh had done the same on this building as the other and I had arranged for it to be set up ready for the machines once production ceased down south. I had decided to use the German injection moulding machines and they were currently on site setting them up, once the first one was in, the robotics team were to follow suit, installing robots and conveyors, racking for the storage of materials and benches were being set up in readiness.

On Monday I was at home on the phone when Martha came in and said a chap called John Nicholls was at the door, in all that had been going on, I had forgotten he was coming, I asked Martha to let him in and then show him to my study. John was like a rabbit in the headlights with the house and it still gave me a buzz of pride to see the expression on someone's face the first time they saw our home. John walked in with Martha in tow and offered John a drink, when Martha had gone to sort out the drinks, I asked John to take a seat while I finished my call. I had just finished it when Martha returned with the drinks and a scone each telling me that Justin was on the phone and wanted a word. I apologised to John and told him to dig in while I took the call. I asked Justin how things were going and how the family were, and we had a little chat when he said that he had called to give me the heads up that the PM was going to visit the site tomorrow and could I be present? I asked what time and we ended the call. I again apologised to John and said I needed to make a quick call and asked his forgiveness. I called Ben and told him the PM would be on site tomorrow and I would be arriving at noon. I asked him to let Brian know and both of them to have a scout around and make sure it was all well, Ben said he would and looked forward to the visit.

I phoned Alison and asked her to hold any further calls unless it was very serious, then turned to John and said let's go. I told John we could both go in my car, and he could leave his at the house and collect it later. We arrived at the new factory and were met by Jonathan who needed a word. I asked John to carry on into the unit and have a look around while I talked to Jonathan. Jonathan said that the tenant had moved out of the second unit and claimed he wanted more compensation and he had told him no, he said that he wanted to talk to me about it. I told Jonathan that I had full confidence in the decisions he made and unless the chap had grounds for complaint to deal with it himself. Jonathan thanked me and we went our separate ways.

I joined John in the factory and he said he could not believe this much could be done in two weeks. He said he could not wait to get stuck in and get it up and running. I explained that the new moulds would be arriving in two weeks and after trials, he should be producing in three. I gave John a key code for the gates to the industrial site and explained how it worked. I asked him how many of the ten staff were prepared to move up and how many wanted to commute, he said they all wanted to move up and had booked a group section with the mortgage advisor I had recommended. Using the financial scale, I had left it with John to work out how much each of the chaps would be compensated; he said it would cost thirty-five grand. Only one owned his own home and as he had inherited from his parents, he was going to rent it out and buy another close to the factory.

John and I travelled back to my home and chatted on the way; he was really excited like a child with a new toy and looking forward to getting stuck in. When we got home, I asked if he wanted to come in for a drink and he said, if it was ok, he would head off back home and inform the lads what to expect. I reminded John to let the lads know that the engineers that had installed the machines would be returning in two weeks-time for three days to go through the machine and explain and sort out any concerns they may have with the unfamiliar equipment. Before he left, I informed him that the injection moulding side of the business would be a trade moulder and I had contacted some of my contacts to see if we could drum up some business and we should know in a few weeks. I told John to get the keys from Jonathan the day before the workforce arrived as I could not give them to him now as we still had engineers working on site. I bid John a safe journey home and went into the house.

After about half an hour, a knock came as I was passing the front door. I opened it and John was standing there, he needed a jump start as his battery was flat. Fortunately, we had a set of jump leads in the garage and while getting him started he told me that it had been playing up for a while but we soon had him on his way. I went back into the house just as dinner was being served. Over dinner, I explained to Julie what we were embarking on and the sequence of events that had caused it to happen. I told Julie about the PM's visit tomorrow and said I would be spending the night down there and would return on Saturday. To my surprise, Julie asked if she could accompany me as she had not seen the site and would like to see it for herself. I thought it a wonderful idea and welcomed her company with delight. We turned in that night early knowing we would be up and out early the next morning.

At six the alarm woke us and we were down by half past, Martha was already in the kitchen and said she knew we were heading out early and did not want us to leave with an empty stomach. Martha was priceless, I could not believe how fortunate we were to have such loyal friends and counted our blessings every day. By seven o'clock we were starting off with a small case each and sandwiches to boot. By now I knew the route without using the satnav and also knew the shortcuts as well. We made really good time and were on site by eleven am. I think everyone was surprised to see Julie and it was nice that they were treating her like royalty. I asked Ben if all was ready for our distinguished guest and he confirmed it was. The bus had been cleaned and everything had been double-checked to make sure nothing went wrong. Expecting the possibility of a large party I asked Ben to bring up the second bus just in case and ensure that it was in good order.

The situation with the coronavirus had once again raised its head, we had a new variant called Omicron and it had come from Africa, it was starting to spread fast, so the need to wear masks on site had been made mandatory again and this included any visitors.

25

Prime Minister's visit

The PM turned up around a quarter past twelve with a whole team of people including about twenty members of the media. In tow were the Energy Minister and Justin, four Housing Ministers, and several more from the meeting we had attended in Downing Street. I greeted the PM and those that accompanied him and introduced him to Ben and Brian the site managers, and Benjamin the site foreman. I then introduced him to Julie and said she would be accompanying us on the tour as she had not seen any of it to date. The PM said he was surprised and asked if she would sit with him for the trip. We all got on board; we had no option other than to use both buses as each one would only seat sixteen. I understood that on the second bus the aisles were full of standing press.

We started the trip by going through phases one and two and explained that once the sewage plant was up and running these houses would be occupied within the next three weeks. The PM asked if we could stop and go into one of the houses and this we did. He was surprised at how much space was available in each room, commenting that in many of the houses he had visited in the past, he said you could not swing a cat around and he openly said he was impressed. We then moved onto the slip road to the wind farm and pulled up at the crest just before the descent to the turbines. This had now all been completed and although not running, they were ready to go. Our next stop was through phase five, the shopping mall; it was still under the final stages of construction but it was very clear the size and design of what was to come. Again, the PM asked us to stop so he could have a walk around and maybe have some photos taken. We must have spent an hour on the one phase and both Julie and I were in some of the photos taken along with Justin and many of the others.

By three o'clock we were just reaching phase four, the treatment plant; it had been finished for some time and the engineers that were installing the plant were all outside to welcome the PM. He was escorted around by the Energy Minister and a couple of advisors and asked when it would be ready. He was told it was all ready to go and I told Justin that it had been tested several weeks ago and the test went well. Justin said he would pass on the information should the subject be raised but not to contradict the Energy Minister for now he would keep it to himself.

The trip back to the central site where the marquees were sited took us through phase six and as we were going through, it was evident from the different stages of development on each house how they were coming together. When we reached the base camp, the PM asked about the three marquees and what their function was. I explained that we used one for the canteen and restaurant and this doubled for film shows in the evening; the other was for sleeping quarters for the workers and the third for storage of items that could be damaged due to bad weather. He asked if he could see the living accommodation and the canteen. I walked him into the living quarters and explained how each person had their own private space and we had underfloor heating, and in the summer months the fans we had rigged up to get through-put of fresh air.

We then went into the restaurant and I asked the PM if he would like to have a meal. His eyes lit up. I explained the menu and waited for him to choose; he skipped the starter and went for a main course and apple pie and ice cream for pudding. He asked how it was paid for and I explained what was available and the costs involved. I also stated it was a non-profit-making system and what was left over from the purchase of the food paid the staff. Once the meal was over, the PM used the opportunity to have photos taken with the kitchen staff to their delight and then thanked them for a wonderful meal. The PM asked where the buses worked from as his motorcade came directly down to the centre of the site. I showed him by explaining that the bus hub and car park were situated on the other side of the storage marquee and once that had been dismantled, the hub and car park would be finished off. The PM was delighted with his visit and congratulated everyone on a super job well done.

As they were all getting back into their cars, the PM stopped, removed his face mask and said to Julie and me, fantastic job, well done. Justin followed behind getting into the same car and just gave the thumbs up and winked his eye. At that, the visit was over and life could return to normal.

The site was busy as most of the workers were coming out of the canteen and either heading back to the accommodation marquee or heading off to the local pub about seven miles away. One of the rules of the site was that no alcohol was allowed; this had happened some time ago when three of the chaps had brought several cases of beer back and been drinking at lunchtime, the chaps were interviewed, and they were told it was a dry site and no alcohol could be consumed there at any time. Brian came over and asked how I felt the visit had gone, I told him that as far as I was concerned it had gone well and the little feedback was encouraging. I would probably get a call later in the evening from Justin but I was not concerned.

We had decided to go for a walk and Julie and I were walking along what was termed the main road to the village which was not more than a single strip of tarmac and my mobile phone rang. As I had expected it to be Justin, I was surprised when Jonathan said hello. I said how are things and he told me he had bought the wood to the rear of the property for one point five million and had to sign a covenant saying that the wood could not be harvested and must remain a wooded area for no less than ninety-nine years. I told Jonathan that I was happy we now owned it and looked forward to exploring it properly on my return when we had a little time. We had only just reached the village when the phone went again, this time it was a sales rep from my past who had heard I was back in the game and had some customers looking for someone to do some moulding for them. I explained I was not at home at the moment and arranged to meet him in Talib's restaurant the following day. We chatted for a few more moments and it was nice to catch up on what had been going on. I thanked him for the call and we carried on with our walk, within fifty yards my phone was going again and the look on Julie's face said it all. I put the phone on voice mail just as we started to head home.

I must say it was nice to be out in the fresh air and I made a conscious decision not to take my phone next time we were trying to have a little 'our time'. As we returned home both Sandra and Bridget were just leaving. Bridget had started working for us part-time in helping Sandra do the housework and between them, they were doing a very good job. We said our goodbyes and went into the house. Martha told us that dinner was ready and that if we went into the dining room, she would serve it up. I asked Martha if she would join us for dinner and she accepted my invitation. Once we were all sitting eating yet again a delicious dinner, I asked Martha how things were with her son Josh. She said that Josh and his wife were having some difficulties and had been for some time. She was worried that their marriage may not survive, and Josh was talking about coming back home. I told Martha that if we could help in any way she only needed to ask, she thanked us and we all got stuck into the washing up.

During the evening, I could not get Martha and Josh out of my mind. Julie told me to leave it alone as it would not do for us to interfere with Martha's private life. I said that I only wanted to help and although Martha was only a few years younger than us, I considered her an extension to the family. Julie said we should wait and that if Martha needed our help, she would talk to us at a later date. While we were talking, the phone rang and it was Justin, he told us that the visit had gone really well and even the opposition to the project was behind what they had seen. He went on the say the PM was overjoyed with the complete programme and asked for his personal thanks to be added when he called me. We both settled down and watched television for the rest of the evening and retired around eleven pm.

The next morning, I was up early and had eaten breakfast by nine am. I told Julie I would be back late evening and headed for the site. I was fifty miles into the journey when I remembered I had arranged a meeting with Colin Wilson about the injection moulding. It was my fault I should have arranged it through Alison and she would have reminded me by putting it in the diary. I called Colin and asked if it was still all set and he said he was putting the last bits and pieces together. I asked where he was and he said he lived in Barnstable and would be leaving for our meeting in about thirty minutes. I asked if I could come to him and would he arrange a pub or restaurant close to his home. Colin said it was ok and he would call me back in an hour with the location.

I arrived at the pub by noon and decided to wait inside. I was quite happy watching the comings and goings of people and Colin turned up a little early. We settled down with a drink and ordered our meal. We were talking about the people we had worked with and companies that had gone to the wall and I asked Colin what had made him go into the line of work he was now in. He explained that he had been made redundant as a lot of plastic companies had gone to the wall and he was unemployed for a while; then he heard about some tooling that needed someone to take on and manufacture; he spoke to a number of people and finally agreed to a contract where he made a nice sum of commission and a percentage of profit from each order. I asked how he was finding the market and he told me that work was scarce as most of the manufacturing had gone abroad but, he had some work available should I be interested. We discussed the work for several hours, including what size machine it would need to be made on, the, numbers required, colours, price, who owned the tools, and dozens of questions until I agreed to have the tools sent to our unit for sampling and pricing.

It was clear by the time Colin and I had finished I was not going to get to the site today so, I started the homeward-bound trip. On the way back I called John and told him to expect a set of eleven tools for sampling on Wednesday and I wanted him to arrange the materials and do the samples as soon as possible. I had advertised in the rubber and plastics papers that we had set up the moulding shop and had a couple of calls from people saying they had work. I had passed on the callers to John and during our conversation, he told me that one of the callers had a suit of seven tools making plastic tents and groundsheet pegs. He had also arranged for these to be sampled and had ordered the material. I asked John what size of orders he would expect, he said they were not huge numbers but, would keep a couple of machines busy for three days of the week. We had two one-hundred, one two-fifty and one four-hundred-tonne machine and I had discussed with the manufacturers to have two more delivered and fitted within a couple of months, it looked like my hunch would pay off. I aimed to have the machines running at eighty per cent capacity and eighty per cent utilisation. I told john that he should do the maths to find out how much spare capacity he would have should we be lucky enough to get all the work we were looking at, I had not told John yet about the two new machines on order.

On the way back home, I decided to go into the moulding factory to see how things were going. The engineers from the machine company had left and our chaps were all at work. I had a good look around and made a few mental notes to bring up with John the next day. John had set up a 104 hours per week operation starting on Monday at seven am and running through to five pm on Friday. We had eight men working on site, nine with John and as we were far from full capacity, the lads could cope quite well. I had a chat with each of the lads to make sure they were well, and the move-up had been successful, they seemed in good spirits and content with the developments to date. I got home around six-thirty and Martha had left me a dinner all plated up; while I was showering Julie warmed it up for me. Feeling tired from all the driving I went into the study to go through a couple of reports that Alison had asked me to peruse.

The next morning, I woke early and decided to have a walk around our new wood. I had walked through it several times over the years we had lived here but never went off the tracks, this was the time to explore. As I entered the wood, I moved off to the right into what appeared to be the thickest part, I found all sorts of trees from oak to elm and mainly silver birch. The larger trees were silver birch and the thickest were the oaks; they must have been here for many years untouched, the circumference was huge, and I could not stretch my arms a quarter of the way around. With the undergrowth, it was clear that the wood had been left to develop on its own, it desperately needed to be cleared of fallen trees and undergrowth. I found lots of signs of deer droppings and rabbit, as well as fox holes and some larger ones that may have been a badger, I wasn't sure.

Not sure what to do I decided to call Brian to see if he had any ideas; he mentioned that one of the guys on site had talked to him about looking for a wooded area that he could live in and off the land. As Brian was telling me about this chap, I remembered him talking to me one day on site about what he would have loved to have been doing. I asked Brian if he could ask the chap to call me so we could discuss it and ended the call. I carried on further into the wood and found what must have been some kids' den, it had fallen into disrepair and clearly not been used in years. Venturing further in I found the remains of an old building, it looked like it must have been an old single-storey cottage many years ago, the roof was missing as were most of the walls. I had a good look around but could not gain anything as to who had lived there. Outside I found an old well, again it had collapsed and was well-grown over.

Moving off I followed an old deer track and found a large circular area with a single oak tree in the centre, scattered around were primulas in the thousands and the area looked beautiful and would have been an ideal place for a picnic. I kept walking and found plenty of mature trees and as I was approaching the end of the wood, I spotted a second property, this one looked a little better than the first one, well at least it had a roof and walls. The front door was missing and as I went in, it looked like it had again been unoccupied for years. I went upstairs to the first floor and found some old magazines dating back to 1943 priced at threepence. On the top corner, I found written in pencil, the name Johnson, the Lodge. The magazine was in good condition so I kept looking. At some time or other, the place had been used by someone looking for shelter as I found old cans and the sign that a fire had been lit in the hearth. I kept searching and found nothing further of interest and I decided to take a different route back home to see if I could find anything else. As I was perhaps halfway back, I came across an area covered in rhododendrons and throughout the wood, bluebells and primulas. I was excited by what I had found and decided that when I returned, I would try to find out about the properties and who lived there, it was quite clear that the wood had remained undisturbed for decades.

It was starting to get dark when I came out of the forest and I found myself down by Julie's kennels. The dogs decided to let everyone know that someone had come through the wood. As I tracked across the grass towards home all I could hear were the dogs barking and this set off the three we had that lived in the house. Martha heard the noise and let our three out and they came charging over the grass to me, it was a nice welcome home. As I entered the house, I had a call from a chap called Blue; his real name was Martin Holmes, he was the chap I had spoken to several months ago on site. I could tell he was on edge being asked to call me and I did my best to alleviate his concerns. I explained to him, what I had seen and asked if he could come up and see the place for himself and advise me on a suitable course of action. I offered to pay his expenses and Blue accepted straight away. He told me he would travel up on the weekend and return the same day. I explained that I would be on site Friday and he could return with me and this would allow us to discuss it further. I would drop him off at the train station when he was ready. That all being agreed, I called Alison and asked if she would be good enough to look into the background of the wood and with the information I had gained, try to find out as much as she could. Alison was just about to leave the office complex and she picked up the little detail I had and said she would do her best.

I went into the house and after saying hi to everyone I went upstairs for a shower. I was very excited about what I had found and seen and was looking forward to telling Julie all about it later during dinner. Once I had showered and come downstairs, Martha said that dinner would be ready in fifteen minutes, this gave me just enough time to book into the local hotel by the site. I felt I had been neglectful for the past couple of weeks and decided to spend the rest of the week on site. During dinner I explained to Julie what my plans were and again to my surprise, she asked to come along.

The next morning both Julie and I left the house at nine am, the plan was that I would drop Julie and our bags off at the hotel and carry on to the site. It was gone lunchtime by the time we booked in and I was eager to get to the site. Julie said she would be having lunch and then going into town to have a look around. I asked if she would drop me off at the site and if she could pick me up later, this being the case, off we went. It had been three months since I had spent any real time on the site and I had full trust in Ben and Brian. The changes were staggering, the treatment plant was up and running, as was the wind farm, and out of the three thousand homes built most were occupied. The hard-standing area we had used for the hub had been completed and the shuttle system was running at full throttle. What I had seen today filled me with pride and excitement. I caught the shuttle bus and was given the full tour around the various sites as part of the drop-off round-robin system. I got off halfway around to walk up to the treatment plant and was amazed at how quiet it was.

Getting on the next shuttle bus, I continued until we reached the wind turbine road. This was quite a long road and a good walk to reach the turbines themselves. I got off and started my trek up the road, I could not hear the turbines until I reached the crest of the hill going down to the coast. Some of the turbines were stationary, while others were moving quite fast. The last fifty metres were fenced off to prevent unwanted visitors, that's not to say it was not available to the public as schools were doing guided tours to both the treatment plant and the turbine farm. The hub area had been finished off early, apart from the final layer of tarmac as with the residents moving into the houses and not having access to be able to drive their cars to their front doors, it was a necessity. Phases seven, eight and nine had been fenced off to keep the children away and I could not see above the fencing to have a look at what stage the houses were in.

As the bus dropped me off at the terminal, I decided to have a walk into the shopping mall and see how this part of the development had progressed. To my surprise, some of the shops were trading and a large coffee shop set out in the middle of the mall had a buzzing business. Having ordered a coffee and bacon sandwich, I walked around searching for a seat, having difficulty finding a vacant one a couple asked if I wanted to sit at their table. I thanked them and we started chatting. I explained that it was the first time I had been in the mall and was looking forward to seeing all the shops open. They told me that the restaurant was excellent and although they had not been in the pub, it apparently was very nice. I asked them how they felt about the new complex and the facilities available and they replied that it was odd not being able to drive directly to their own homes and having to catch the bus for the last bit, but it was something they were prepared to do in order to live here. They said that the new electric cars coming out were getting cheaper and that in the next couple of years, they would be able to afford one themselves. They also told me that they felt that they were in the first stage of a pioneering development that would be extended across the world and felt privileged to be part of it. I asked about the price of the house and did they feel comfortable in it. They said the house had cost £315,000 and although they had stretched themselves, they knew that they did not have to worry about large electricity bills anymore and in fact were expecting a cheque every three months for the excess their home sold to the national grid. They told me that because the entire town was considered a green town the local council had charged all houses as category A, being the lowest rate for a home available.

They asked if I lived in the town or was thinking of buying here, and I explained that I was just having a good look around and had not come to any decision. They told me that they had moved up from Cornwall last month and were one of the first to move in, they said they loved the whole concept and had been visited by members of their family who had kids and they had spent hours in the parks and just walking around. They were now considering moving up and had put their house on the market and their name down on one of the houses in phase nine. I thanked the couple for letting me use their table and telling me about their experience. I left the couple to finish their coffee in peace and decided to carry on walking around the mall.

Out of the thirty shops, a third were trading and it looked like another ten were on the verge of opening. From what I could see, there would be two cafes or coffee shops, two quite small supermarkets at the bottom of the mall, a pet shop, a pharmacy, a florist's, a bank, a post office, a D.I.Y shop, a lighting shop, and shops to come included a carpet shop, a sign and graphics shop, footwear, a travel-agents, alcohol, a solicitor's and several more I could not make out. When I got outside, I decided to walk over to the large supermarket, it was up and running and the place was quite full. The supermarket chain that had taken on the shop had been restricted in what they could sell, they were told they could not sell, electrical goods, clothing, D.I.Y, flowers, pharmacy items, currency, travel, live-stock, these had been put in place to prevent the large dominating superstore from putting out of business all the smaller business. They could sell meat, newspapers, fish, fresh food and sanitary items, this had all been set up to allow the smaller shops the opportunity to survive against an overpowering superstore. We had all seen how the superstores were killing the high street traders and did not want it to happen here.

I had noticed during my time walking around that there were no builders or garden centres and this gave me the idea that I might be able to use one of the marquees we currently used and do what we did on phase one's development and split it into two halves; it was something to consider for the future. Up until now, I had not been interested in taking over any of the shops or parts of the mall and all of a sudden, I felt we had missed a trick. We had been so involved in the development and not seen a golden opportunity to advance the business and now it may be too late. I would talk to a few people and see how the land lay.

I returned just as Julie had pulled up at the bus terminal and we started to head for the hotel. I told her what I had seen. I agreed that before we started back on Friday evening, we could pick up Blue and before that, I would show her around using the buses. I asked how her day had gone and she told me that all the talk in the local villages was about the new town and how it was developing, several of the shops were moving to the new complex and had signs up telling customers they were moving in the next couple of weeks to new locations and giving their new address. We reached the hotel and booked in, once in and settled we headed for the restaurant. I was quite well known by the staff now and knew most of them by name. We ordered dinner and a drink to start with.

We were just finishing our dinner when a chap I had not spoken to before came over and introduced himself as the owner and manager of the hotel. He asked if we would mind if he joined us and we of course agreed. Once he was sitting, he explained that due to the development of the town and all the people coming to visit and stay at his hotel he had been able to purchase a second hotel in Plymouth. He said that he had hoped I would come into the hotel again so he could thank me personally and say thank you for our stay today and our meal was on the house. We were surprised, to say the least, and thanked him for his generosity. We continued to chat for a couple of hours and as it was too late to go out decided to spend a couple of hours in the bar before retiring. Phillip joined us and we continued to chat for several more hours, finally going to bed around one am.

The next morning, Thursday, I asked Julie if she would drop me off at the site and she could have the car for the day; this we did and I was on site by ten am having had a good full breakfast. As I was on foot and wearing my hi-vis and hard hat and boots, I walked around quite freely and ended up at Ben's portacabin, having knocked on the door it was opened by one of the builders and I asked if it was ok to come in. The chap recognised me and invited me in. Ben was surprised to see me and was shocked that I had managed to get to his porta cabin without him hearing I was on site. I told Ben that I had come down the day before and had used the buses to have a tour around the complex. I explained that what I had seen was very encouraging and also told him about my coffee in the mall yesterday. Ben again said he was amazed that I had been floating around all day without him being told and started to explain the new phases they were working on. Ben told me that they were on target to come in three years ahead of the original target and phases seven, eight, nine and eleven were all currently being worked on.

The system Ben had used in keeping a small team of eight chaps together under their own charge hand and only bringing in specialists if needed or extra labour had worked really well. We knew that we were going to come in before the scheduled date for the whole development but, I was very surprised when Ben said it would be three years early. I asked Ben how he felt about finishing the project before he retired as he was due to retire at the end of this year, as we had agreed five years ago. Ben said that he would talk to his better half at the weekend and let me know on Monday. As we were talking, Brian walked in hearing that I was on site and he too had been surprised he had not heard about my presence. We joked about me keeping an eye on them and said I had a checking device so they had better watch out. I asked both Ben and Brian if one of them had time to show me around the new phases and both said they would love to.

We set off on foot and were in phase seven within ten minutes. Out of the one thousand houses in this phase, over half were built and all the others were in various stages ranging from just the slab to having the roof fitted. None of the houses could be sold on any phase until the last house was complete and the roads and pavement system were complete. Walking onto phase eight, the slabs were all down and forty-six of the houses were complete, again many in various stages of the build. Phase nine only had the slabs down and phase eleven only had footings currently being poured. Nevertheless, what Ben and Brian had achieved was nothing short of a miracle and I told them both that I was extremely thankful and proud of what they had achieved. We walked back to the porta cabin and I asked if both Ben and Brian would join Julie and me at the hotel so I could buy them both dinner tonight as a little thank you. Both agreed and we set a time for seven pm. By five pm, I call Julie to pick me up and told her we would be having guests for dinner tonight. I arrived back at the hotel with just enough time to have a shower and change before Ben and Brian arrived.

After dinner, we talked about our families and how the continuous nonstop pressure of the builds had impacted our lives and that of our families. I said that it had been a driving force for me and I could not have rested even if I had wanted to. Ben said that he had enjoyed the past fifteen years and would not change any of it for the world, he had become more wealthy working with me than he ever thought possible and could now look forward to a retirement with ease and no financial problems. Brian said he would be glad when this current project was over as he had missed his wife and kids a lot and would spend some time with them before starting any other projects. I said to Brian that this most likely would be the biggest project he would ever work on, and he should be very proud that he had been instrumental in its development from such an early stage through to the conclusion.

At the end of the evening, I thanked both for coming and Julie and I retired to our room. It had been an enjoyable evening with two good friends and it was nice to know that they both had enjoyed the journey that we had all shared together. I spent the next day on site shadowing Ben and discussing various points after Julie had dropped me off. She had gone into the shopping mall to look for herself and would return to pick me and Blue up around four pm.

At lunchtime, Ben and I went into the marquee for lunch and Brian joined us; it was nice to see that the standard of the meals had not dropped off. While we were having lunch, I watched one of the chaps pull a hip flask from his pocket and pour the contents into his soft drink. I quietly leaned over to inform Ben and he said he would deal with it. As we got up to leave Ben asked the chap to come to the office after lunch and we walked out. Brian and I had decided to go and have a look around phase seven and left Ben to deal with the issue of what I had seen. Just over an hour later we returned to the porta cabin and Ben said that the chap had gone, he claimed he had been drinking rum since his arrival and it had not impaired his ability to date, Ben had to explain to him that it was a dry site without exceptions and that his contract was terminated with immediate effect and had agreed to pay him until the end of the month. Ben had walked him off-site and informed security that he was not allowed on site again without an escort and then only to see himself or Brian.

26

The wood

Julie returned to the site having packed our belongings and loaded the car. Blue and I were both waiting and climbed in and I introduced Blue to Julie. Julie was driving and Blue sat in the back. I turned around so we could talk. I explained to Blue why I had asked him to come and have a look at the wood and wanted his opinion as to what to do. I told him about the two derelict buildings and that I was trying to find out what I could about the history of the place. I asked Blue to tell me about himself and he said that he had left school at sixteen with no prospects and no qualifications and had started as a labourer on our first build. When we started the second build, he had progressed to chippy and could almost put his hand to anything. I asked what his long-term plans were and he said that they were a little unclear after his current job finished but felt he would never be out of work. The original plan was that we were going to drop Blue off at the bed and breakfast place but Alison had forgotten to make the call so I asked Blue if he would mind roughing it at our place tonight. He agreed and we pulled up at nine pm. The traffic back had been horrendous and it seemed the drive was never-ending.

To our surprise, Martha had decided to stay over and had cooked a meal ready for our return. I could see the look on Blue's face and told him to relax. I showed him to his room and said dinner would be ready in twenty minutes. I was just coming out of the study when Blue was walking down the stairs, he followed me into the dining room and we had a lovely meal. I could see that Blue was uncomfortable and asked if he would like a tour around the house, as we went from room to room, I explained to Blue that we had not always lived like this and I could see him start to relax. I asked if he played snooker and he said he had a little. For a flash second, I thought this might be someone I could beat. WRONG. We played four games and although I did myself proud, he still won three of them.

The next morning, we were up for eight and sitting in the dining room when Blue walked in. I asked if he had slept well and he said like a log. After breakfast, we started our walk into the woods, I showed Blue all I had seen and asked what he thought; he told me that the wood had been neglected for years and that the one building at the far end could be salvaged but it would take a lot of time and money. I asked Blue what was the best solution to getting the wood to a decent standard and could a living be made from it. Blue thought for a while and said, if it were him doing the job, he would camp out by the derelict building and providing he could afford the materials, do it up over a period of time. He would need to clear a lot of dead wood off the floor and cut down some of the diseased and dying trees. Once this was done someone could make a small living by making firewood and things from the wood itself. He said he would turn it into a training camp for kids to give them the experience of the great outdoors and living off the land. He said that it would take years to put all this together and the cost would run into the thousands spread over a few years. I told Blue why we had bought the wood in the first place to secure our rear boundary and Blue said that that could be secured by putting a solid fence across say fifty metres in with sensors on, and a gate could be installed so access could be maintained should we wish to walk into the wood.

I asked Blue to expand on what he said about living off the land. He said that providing it was an option, he could clear some of the land for crops and as he was good with his hands, he could make things out of the wood he salvaged from the wood itself. These could be sold and the money would purchase the items he could not make or grow himself. I asked Blue if he would consider taking on the project if he were offered, and he replied without hesitation that he would love to. I asked what assets he would bring to the table and he said that money was not his worry as he had been left a small trust fund from a previous life, you could not live off it on its own but, doing what he had suggested would work. I told Blue that we would have enough materials around to build the derelict building back up but access would be the biggest problem as it would all have to go through the wood itself. He said he had seen a small track leading to a farm track that if the owner would allow access, he could use from the other end of the wood.

I was excited by what Blue had said about turning it into a get-away for kids to get back to nature, and decided that I wanted Blue to head up the task. I asked him if he would accept my offer of providing the materials he needed to build the derelict back up, and I would finance the project for twelve months to get it started. I would approach the farmer who owned the land at the rear of mine and see if we could sort something out. Blue asked when he could start and I said that with what he had in mind working with children, we would have to do a DBS check on him. This is the Disclosure and Barring Service, formerly known as the CRB, Criminal Records Bureau, which anyone wanting to work with children has to submit to, to make sure they don't have any former convictions etc which may make them a danger to children. I asked if the DBS check would raise anything and he assured me it would be ok.

I also told Blue that Ben had said he was very good at what he did and he did not want to be without his skill, so this would not start until the existing project was coming to an end, and this would be around eighteen months to two years. Blue said that he understood what I was saying and wanted this more than anything, he would wait as long as it took for the opportunity as this is what he had dreamt of for years. I thanked him for his input and after dinner, I took him back to the railway station. As he was leaving to get on the train, he said that he was really enthusiastic and thanked me for the opportunity he had been offered. Martha had packed Blue a lunch for his return journey and I wished him a safe journey.

I returned home and straight away was on the phone. I called Dave and asked him to come and see me the next day with Alison and then looked for the number of the farmer that owned the land to our rear. I was just about to call him having searched for over an hour when Julie came in and asked what I was doing. I explained that I was just about to make a call when she said, did I realise it was almost eleven o'clock? It had not registered with me and I was surprised. We went into the living room and had some tea and a scone before going to bed an hour later.

The next morning Dave and Alison came as requested to see me, I asked Alison to do a DBS check on Martin Holmes, alias Blue, and said she could find his file in the labour recruited for the southern development. I pulled a map out and showed Dave where I wanted an eight-foot palisade fence installed and linked up to our existing boundary fencing. I then call Robert Barnes and asked if he had a little time to have a look at extending our security. He said he would be down in the hour. I went in to join Julie at breakfast and by the time I had finished, Robert was at the gate. I buzzed him in and met him at the front door. It was nice to see Robert as I had not laid eyes on him for several months having spent a lot of time down south. I asked him to follow me into the study where I had a map showing the area, I wanted to secure. I explained that Dave would be doing the fencing and said I wanted some sort of sensor that would not pick up wildlife but would pick up people should they enter from the wooded area. Robert suggested adding two more cameras to the rear of our home and razor wire to the top of the fence, in addition, he suggested a system that could not be seen by the naked eye but would run just behind the fence and it would detect any movement and as it was high up on the fence, no wildlife would set it off.

While Robert and I were discussing this, Dave came in saying he had sufficient fencing left over from the first industrial park and could start installing it tomorrow and it would take one week. I told Robert he had a week to organise what we had discussed. For the rest of the morning, we just sat in the study talking and Robert asked all about what we had been working on for the past few years. Once the second stage build had been completed, Dave had stayed most of the time up north helping Jonathan and had had little to do with the southern project, so what I was telling Robert was equally interesting to Dave.

After Dave and Robert had left, I had a call from Ben and he said that he had had Blue in his office telling him all about his weekend and my proposal. He told him that he did not wish to lose the opportunity to grasp the offer with both hands and wanted to know if there was any way he could walk away from this role down south early and take up the new role on offer. I told Ben we were not ready to start the project just yet and also told him that I thought it would be eighteen months to two years before he could release him. Ben explained that Blue was exceptional with his skills and it would be hard to replace him, and the decision to do so was for him to make, he did not wish to sway him in any direction. Ben thanked me for not putting him under further pressure and said he would look at the situation next week and see what he could do.

I had put a call in to my neighbour that morning and was awaiting a call back that came just after lunch. I introduced myself and explained why I was calling. I arranged to meet Phillip later that afternoon at the far end of the wood. After dinner, I started to walk through the wood and could not get over how beautiful all the wildflowers and trees were. I met Phillip Gold as arranged at 2 pm and shook hands. I had been meaning to go and see him to introduce myself for no other reason than to say hi for quite some time and felt guilty that I had not done so. He was a tall man maybe six-three and just as broad with silver hair and aged about fifty. I apologised for not meeting with him earlier and explained why I had asked for our meeting today. He looked concerned that the peace and tranquillity he had enjoyed for so long would be shattered by a lot of kids running around breaking fences and causing mayhem. I went into detail about what I envisaged for the area and said I felt it would not come out of the wood, as once they had entered, the whole idea was that they would live off the land for the week or two that they were on site. I explained that the one ruin would be restored for safety as much as anything and a refuge in the worst of weather. Once everyone was in the wood and the supplies were in place, I would hope he would not know they were there.

Phillip's farm was a smallholding of fifty acres and he himself used it as a petting farm and refuge for all sorts of animals rescued by the RSPCA and other institutions. He was funded by charitable contributions and selling the odd recovered duck that could not fly or the pony that was healthy but blind in one eye. The track that Blue had seen was not used and ran along the top field of his rescue farm. I asked if it was possible to rent the land from him so we could gain access or if that did not work for him, maybe we could purchase the track. Phillip said he could do with the income from both proposals and asked what figure I had in mind. I explained that the track covered around one acre in total and that for any inconvenience I would round the figure up to ten thousand pounds and cover the legal fees for both of us in signing over the land. Phillip agreed on the spot and I said I would draw up a contract of sale and if he would like to come to the house next Monday, I would have it ready to sign.

We both went our separate ways. I called our solicitors and asked Paul Webb to pop into our house when he had a little time. That evening Paul was at the gate and I buzzed him in and met him at the front door. We went into the study; I had not spoken to him since he drew up the contract with the government five years ago. Once we were seated and Martha had supplied us with drinks and a scone, I explained what I had been doing and what I needed him to do. I also said that I wanted him to draw up a contract for Blue. I made it very clear that it should read that Martin Holmes, alias Blue, must be responsible for all aspects of health and safety and must have the appropriate public liability insurance in place at all times and we would not accept any liability for loss of life, injury or property. I also said that to ensure our company was protected, I would rent the land to Martin on an annual basis for one pound a year. Paul understood and said he would have it ready by Friday and drop it down for my perusal. He spent the rest of the afternoon with me and I found his news about the local parish council interesting. He said that since Justin and Robert had left the council to their own devices, it had gone downhill and needed a new influx of energy and drive. I said that Paul himself should stand for election and that would shake them up; he turned around and said he was thinking more about me. I laughed and said I was getting too old and could not stand the slow pace of politics. I asked him to stay for dinner and he gladly accepted. It was gone ten o'clock before he left and it had been an enjoyable visit. By the end of the day, I had arranged what I considered a suitable candidate for looking after the wood, secured the access, and arranged for the DBS check on Blue and the contract to be drawn up; what council could do that in one day?

By the end of the week, Paul dropped off the contracts and told me he had considered what we discussed about his standing for the council and had decided to go for it. I told him he would have my vote and that if I could help in any way, let me know. I could not think of a better candidate than Paul to take on such a role; he was honest, smart and determined to see things through, just what the council could do with. Paul left the contracts with me and on Saturday morning Dave came into my study to explain that he had almost completed the fencing and it would be ready on Monday. I told him well-done and we settled down for a couple of games of snooker.

While we were playing, Ben came in saying he had found a replacement for Blue and that I could have him next month if I still wanted him. As Jonathan was already in the house emptying our kitchen of food, he joined us for a foursome on the snooker table; I joined with Dave and Jonathan with Ben. Dave and I lost; I obviously needed to take up a different hobby. When we had finished, I gave Ben the contract I had drawn up for Blue and asked him to pass it along and if Blue was happy, sign and return the documents. As everyone was leaving, Phillip Gold arrived. I buzzed him through and went into the study. Jonathan brought Phillip in, I stood and shook hands and offered him a drink. He asked for a Scotch and Jonathan did the deed. Phillip said that he remembered this house before we moved in and always wanted to see it for himself. I asked if he would like to have a tour around and he jumped at it. We left Jonathan in the study and set off into the hall.

Thirty minutes later, we were back and I explained that I had drawn up the contract for Phillip to peruse and if he was happy with it, to sign in his own time. He looked through it quite quickly and signed it. I asked if he was sure he was happy and wouldn't prefer to take it away and get his solicitor to go through it with him. Phillip surprised both Jonathan and me by saying he used to be a solicitor working in Paul's firm and knew that Paul would not be a party to anything that was not healthy. I wrote out a cheque for Phillip and the deed was done. We sat chatting for some time about why Phillip had left his career and gone into his present occupation and what we were about to undertake with the wood and by the time we had finished chatting, it was almost midnight. Phillip thanked me for the hospitality and we all said good night.

The next morning, I called Dave and asked if he would be good enough to start collecting the materials we would need to rebuild the derelict and if he was happy to help, give Blue a hand getting the rebuild going. On Sunday I decided to take a drive down to the factory and just check it out. I knew it would not be open but I had a set of keys and wanted to see how it had been left on Friday. I entered the unit and was a little concerned about the lack of cleanliness and by the time I was finished looking around was quite angry with what I could see. Sitting outside in my car, I decided to call John and inform him of my displeasure when he came around the corner. I jumped out of the car and could see the surprise on his face. I told him what I had found and he said that he had gone to see a colourist on Friday afternoon and had left the closing down of the site to Simon.

We went into the factory and I showed him what I had seen and said it was not to happen again; I wanted to trust him and he assured me he would deal with it and it wouldn't happen again. I could see the disappointment on John's face and knew that he felt he had let me down. I left him to it and started back home. On the way, I had a drive around the two industrial sites and was shocked to see caravans parked up outside two of the units and various packaging and stocks being stored outside. I called Jonathan and explained that these were breaches of the agreements and that it could not and would not be acceptable under any circumstances. I wanted it gone by the end of the day Monday and those who were responsible given warnings that should it happen again, they would be evicted. Jonathan was shocked and said he had been around both industrial sites the week before last and neither had these issues. Jonathan said he would be on it Monday morning and it would be sorted by the end of the day. I knew that Jonathan would be good to his word and left him to his own devices.

I returned home and decided to have a walk around the estate. This was something I had taken to when I wanted to think about things. It troubled me that I had had a go at Jonathan but, at the same time, it would remind him to keep on his toes and not become complacent. I knew that

Jonathan was good at what he did and would not be upset by me checking up on things myself. He was experienced enough to know that a second pair of eyes was not a bad thing.

27

Phases 12/13/14

The years passed and we were finally approaching the last phases of the development. Phase eleven was completed just before Christmas and we had simultaneously started on all three of the last phases. We expected to complete the whole project by the end of the year or at the latest the beginning of next year. Ben decided to see the project through and I must say I was glad when he said he would; it was not a concern that Brian would not have done a fantastic job and I know he would have done, but by having Ben leading one group and Brian leading the second and a third group led by the two of them, we were moving at a phenomenal rate.

I had been summoned to a meeting in London several weeks ago which Justin chaired. It had been called to see if it was feasible to extend the town further and almost double its size. Some preliminary plans had been drawn up and we went into detail far more than I thought we would as this was the first meeting scheduled. Behind the scenes, a lot of work had been done by architects and planners alike and I felt I was being drawn into this at a very late date. No conclusion arose from the meeting and I kept my mouth shut as much as possible. When the meeting finished, I asked Justin if I could have a word in private.

Five minutes later the room was ours and I asked him what was going on. He apologised for not briefing me more thoroughly and said that it was most likely that we were about to have a change of government and all parties were looking at making favourable headway by being able to claim they had extended and developed this project. He told me that our current PM had gained so much credit and goodwill from this development, he could do with some additional support and this would go a long way to helping. I said to Justin that from the off I had no intention of getting into the politics and this felt like I was being drawn into something I did not want. He assured me that it was not the case and said that the larger political parties were positioning themselves ready for the next election and his party were getting pieces into place as part of that strategy. He said he had understood from the off that I did not want to get embroiled in politics and he would make sure that this did not happen. I trusted him and took him at his word but I would be keeping my ears and eyes open from now on just in case.

Justin said that his gut feeling was that this further development would not happen in the long term but he was obligated to see it through to a conclusion either way. I told him the news that the project would be completed by the end of this year or early next and he was shocked to hear it; he honestly thought we would come in behind schedule. I asked him about a project that Jonathan had been working on for a while in the background; he had seen a loophole or a shortage of industrial facilities in the area of the town and had purchased a site that was currently derelict some two miles to the west, intending to build an industrial site. The site had been an old power station and covered about twenty-eight acres. Justin said he had already raised the issue with the Environment and Industries Ministers earlier in the month and they all agreed it would need to be looked at. I asked if we were to submit plans for the development and use the systems we had introduced to date, would he support it? He said he felt quite sure that not only would he support it but the entire cabinet would be behind it.

Justin apologised by saying that he would not be able to take me out tonight as he had just been told he had to be in Brussels by nine o'clock tomorrow morning for a meeting and had to prepare for the trip. I said it was fine and I would be heading back home after we had finished. I then invited Justin and the family to come and spend a week or two at Donbecnie. He said he would love to but could not get away for several weeks; as soon as a break in his diary came up he would give us a call.

I planned to head back home but then I thought about the new development and decided to go and see Ben at the site. It was starting to get late and while I was travelling, I called the hotel we often stayed at and booked a room for the night. I then called Julie and put her in the picture. After that, I called Ben and asked if he could join me for dinner at the hotel as I had something to discuss. We arranged a time and I continued with my journey, arriving just after eight pm. Ben was in the bar waiting for me and as soon as I had put my overnight bag in the room, I joined him in the restaurant. We both ordered and while waiting I asked him how Tom was doing. He looked at me as if to say what's going on? I said again, how's Tom doing? Ben said he was doing well and had become a good asset to the company. I told Ben that I had been thinking about Tom for a while and felt with Ben's approval it was time to grow him more. With himself retiring soon and Brian heading up the current and future tasks, he would need additional support and if Tom was ready for more responsibility, it was time to develop his ability. Ben asked what I had in mind. I said that while we were all looking at the current development, Jonathan had been looking at it from the outside and had spotted something we had all missed, industrial units. I saw the recognition register on Ben's face and he nodded. I told him that Jonathan had purchased a site two miles west, an old derelict power station covering twenty-eight acres. If he agreed, Tom could head up its development under his and Brian's guidance and when he retired, both Brain and Tom would be capable of taking on anything between them. I told Ben that although I had not discussed this with anyone else, I intended to retire when Ben did and just stay in the background and attend the occasional board meeting; I would be handing over the reins to Jonathan and the girls.

Ben's face said it all, he was glowing with pride that I had considered his son worthy of advancement at such an early age of just twenty-five. I told Ben that Brian had proved himself to be an excellent project manager and from what I had seen of Tom, he would just follow suit. Our dinner arrived and we continued to discuss the course we would take in developing Tom and assisting him to grow into the role. This current project would be finished by the time Tom would have got the ground works complete, and that was providing planning went through within the year. With Ben retiring, I would draw Brian back to our base awaiting the next project and helping Tom if he should need it and that would give our company a two-edged sword for the future. We decided to keep it between ourselves for the time being and I questioned whether Ben's pride would make him say anything. I must say, I would have understood if he did, but I had realised years ago that Ben could be very discrete and professional when needed.

The next morning before I left for home, I asked the sales office how the sales were going and was told that they were selling as fast as they were released for sale. The two-bedroomed houses were being sold for £280,000, three bedrooms were selling for £315,000 and four bedrooms with one garage selling for £430,000; and two garages for an additional £10,000. Only one house had not been sold; the buyer pulled out and it was resold a further twice and was still going through the legal progress and all the rest were sold. The three next phases were not available for sale to move into until the phase they were on was complete, however, out of the 1,500, 836 were sold off plan. I was surprised and a little shocked and asked what sales technique they had used. They said it was the fact that they would not be getting electricity bills, but instead receiving a small income of £300 plus, per year from the national grid. The houses were the most advanced ever built for heating and comfort and to top it all, security was a high priority; knowing that the cameras and security guards would be patrolling regularly, the sales team said they were selling themselves.

I travelled home that evening feeling high, this could not have been better news. On the way home the traffic was horrendous and it took six hours to get there. On the radio, it said that there had been an accident and when I got to the point where I thought the accident had happened, nothing was visible. On my arrival, the house was all quiet and in darkness and I was looking forward to having a shower and relaxing for the evening. I had been in the house for a couple of hours when Julie walked in saying she had been down at the kennels tending to the dogs and getting them ready for a visit tomorrow for the selection of the latest litter. It was the first time I had been in the house on my own for years and it became apparent to me how big it was. I had made myself a sandwich and was sitting in my study reading some reports when Julie came in and asked if I wanted anything else. I said I was fine and said I would join her in the living room shortly to watch some television. Before she left, she told me that Blue had called and asked when I had time, if could I pop by to see him. By now it was too late but I would walk down tomorrow; I was looking forward to seeing how he had got on with the house and what he had been doing with the wood and the development of the living wild theme.

Julie and I retired around eleven pm and I was up early the next morning sitting in the kitchen with Martha, eating a bacon sandwich when she came down to join us. After breakfast, I started my walk down to see Blue, and as I passed through the gate straight away, I noticed the difference, lots of the fallen branches and undergrowth had been removed; Blue had put loads of bird boxes in the trees of all sizes and they were busy with birds flying in and out, clearly breading was going well. The first thing I found was the derelict building that had just been nothing more than a base and little else, had been tidied up and a wooden structure had been erected forming a bird hide. I carried on walking and ended at the house Blue and Dave had worked on. I was amazed to see the progress he had made. The cottage was finished and he had started to build a porch the full length of the building. In addition, he had built rip slides and assault course-type structures; on the one side he had a working area he must be using for making some of the things scattered around the cottage. He had sculpted badgers, foxes, rabbits, birds, and a huge owl sat in pride of place in the centre of the yard.

As I was standing taking it all in, Blue came up behind me and asked what I thought. I was thrilled, to say the least. I was stuck for words and Blue asked if I wanted a cup of tea. I stammered thanks and followed him into the cottage. He had it set out with little in the way of soft furnishings but lots of things he had made from the wood. The bed, chairs, table, cupboards and shelves were his own making. I told Blue I was amazed at what he had done and asked what his plans were. He said that he had gained permission to run classes for some local school for troubled kids in getting back to nature classes; he had agreed to take kids from twelve to sixteen, both boys and girls and teach them about the beauty of nature and show them how to relax and enjoy a different side of life. He had to show several people what he had done and what he would be teaching and for the first twelve months, he would be monitored by a chaperone until they were confident in him and the programme.

He showed me some of the things he had ready for his first class in two weeks; it included woodworking classes, tracking, identification of birds, trees and plants, enjoying the assault course and relaxing. I was impressed with what Blue had achieved and told him so. He said that for the first twelve months, he would not be paid for the classes but, if it was deemed to be popular and effective, he would get paid for each student that attended the class which could lead to overnight classes and that would be a whole new experience for the kids.

The tea was different and I was looking forward to a proper cup when I got back home, but at least Blue seemed to like it. He told me that he was considering setting up a paintball game where he could use the other derelict building as a centre fort and set two teams against each other and this would bring in needed revenue. I was thrilled to see what Blue had achieved and told him so and asked if he needed my help he only need ask. I started my walk back to the gate and marvelled at the way the wood had come to life. Blue had cleared many of the fallen trees and cleaned up much of the shrubbery that had become overgrown and it was now a beautiful area to walk through. When I got back to the gate, I could not see straight away the additional security Robert had installed and was satisfied that anyone coming through the gate would not see it either.

I had made an appointment with John from the injection moulding and blow moulding unit to come and update me on the progress of the factory and he had been waiting for over an hour by the time I arrived back. I had not realised how long I had been away and apologised for being late. John had been sitting in the reception area and I asked him to follow me into my study so we could go through what he had to say. After Martha had sorted out a drink for us, he said that the work I had brought in a few months ago had been completed and it had been a little disappointing as the numbers required had never come. However, the main company we had been doing the work for had asked us to sample a larger set of tools and these had been for white goods and the numbers were in the tens of thousands. On the blow moulding side of the business, he had received several new customers in the States, Canada and three countries in Europe, the numbers were staggering and they were struggling to meet demand. I had expected this market to grow but did not anticipate the speed of the growth and asked John if he felt we would need to look at a second set of tooling. He said that at the moment our lead time was several weeks and looked like it would become longer very fast. If we did develop a second set of tooling, we would need a second set of machines to run it on. I told John I would order a second set of tooling and another two machines for the blow moulding unit. John had increased production to 120 hours a week and this would give us a further 48 hours if we started to work weekends. I told him to set this up on the blow moulding plant and do it using overtime until he had recruited new staff once the delivery and installation of the new tooling and machines were confirmed.

John and I went through the figures and it appeared the factory was doing very well; the advantage we had was that in the blow moulding side of the business, the tooling was our own design and this gave us a lot of control. As of yet, no one had copied our design and as ours was a proven development, it would take a couple of years for a serious competitor to produce and develop a functional alternative that worked as well as ours. The orders coming in were good and once the countries started to use the system, I knew that the figures would explode.

I asked John how Billy was doing and he told me that he had stopped drinking and gambling and had got his life back on track. I asked if he was ready to come back to work and John said he would love to come back, but John said he felt he was not ready yet and needed more time. I told him to keep me informed. I knew Billy had a good feel for the business and knew that as he did not own the business, the pressure would be off and that might make a huge difference. I felt that in time a second chance would be good for him, but it would be one I would keep my eye on for some time if he did ever come back at all.

John had left about an hour when Robert arrived with Kelly. Martha buzzed him through and we spent the afternoon all talking in the living room. I updated both Kelly and Robert on events; I had not realised how long it had been since we had all been together as a group, which was when we were on holiday in Donbecnie almost two years ago. Robert's firm had grown and had gained a respectable reputation on its own merit. He had quoted for the security of the town we had been building and awarded some of the contract. I had arranged to spend a week at Donbecnie with Justin and his family and asked if Robert and Kelly would like to join us for the week. Robert said they would love to; he and Justin had known each other for years before I came into the picture and had a lot in common. I was looking forward to the week with good company. The family had started to use Donbecnie on a regular basis and it was a question of having to book a space in the calendar if you wanted to spend any time there.

Two weeks later, we were all on holiday. We had all managed to fly out at the same time on the same flight and booked a minibus to take us to our destination. The place was full, with Danie and Jake and the twins, Justin and Sally and the boys, Robert and Kelly and Julie and I. We spent the week relaxing and going to the local theme park, ordering takeaways and swimming in the pool. The couple that looked after the place for us came by a couple of times to resupply us with food and clean towels and we invited them to join us on one of the evenings for cocktails. By the end of the week, we were all a little browner and the worse for wear from too much food and drink. None of us wanted to return to our various places of work and although our phones had been going nonstop, we had all resisted the pull to return home, but home it must be and on Sunday evening, we all packed up and headed for the airport.

28

Coming to an end

The town was now complete and all the houses occupied; it was running very smoothly, the government had kept its promises and paid my company more than what we had originally discussed, as the figure did not include the sales of the mall and entertainment buildings. Both housing estates we had developed were with the malls and industrial estates were bringing in a very good income. The other businesses we had set up over the years were all doing well. I had decided that it was time for me to hand over the reins and step back from the daily running of the business, although I would always maintain a foothold and keep abreast of how things were going. We were due for our next board meeting on Monday morning and I had a lot to prepare prior to making any announcements. On Monday morning, we all assembled in the board room and I opened the meeting by thanking everyone for the efforts to date and for attending this morning. We went through the meeting and as each person delivered their report, we discussed it in detail and talked about solutions and timing scales for resolution. Brian had returned and had taken over Ben's old duties of overseeing the farm buildings and helping Tom when needed, and the site he was working on had advanced well with little guidance from Brian. Tom had proven to be capable and professional just like his dad and brother. Donna had become more involved in the business, taking over many of Becky's duties as Becky had purchased a smallholding and had been working three days a week looking after it. Danie had developed the health centre and had installed some very good managers and could now take a back seat to the daily running. Jonathan had established himself well, while I had been working on the development of the town and he did not need any advice or guidance from me; he was doing a fine professional job and I knew that he would continue to grow the business at an admirable rate.

As everyone had finished going through their report, I said I had an announcement to make and it would have an effect on all of them. All ears pricked up and I told them that I intended to step back from running the company at Christmas and hand over the reins in the following manner: Jonathan would become Managing Director; Donna, Becky and Danie would become Directors and if a vote on a major decision could not be resolved with a two-two vote on policy or asset sales, I or Julie would be brought in and carry the casting vote. I said that Julie and I would continue to live in our home and the offices would continue to be the hub of the business; I would still occasionally attend board meetings to keep in touch with the business. We went through salaries and what I expected from each of them and asked if anyone had a problem with what I had said. With no one raising any concerns I closed the meeting and asked to speak to Jonathan alone.

Once everyone had left, I addressed Jonathan and said that the reins were now in his hands. I had indicated to him several months ago that this would happen and said I had full confidence in his ability to carry the company forward. He said he was a little concerned about the two-two vote system and felt he should have the casting vote in such a situation. I agreed with him and said that on the day-to-day running, he would have, it would only come into force in the event of a company shift in position, such as branching into new fields or selling of current assets. This way it kept the company in the direction I had intended and should Jonathan decide it needed a change, then I would have the opportunity to have my say should I agree with his decision. If I did not, it was up to Jonathan to convince me that I was wrong and that the company would benefit from the change.

We had three weeks till Christmas and Julie was preparing a retirement party for both Ben and me. Jill, Ben's wife was deeply involved in the preparations and both Ben and I kept out of the way. I spent some of my time at Ben's home keeping a low profile and it allowed me to have a look at the houses we had built in Millionaire Row all those years ago. I had only been to Ben's house a couple of times to pick him up and had never stayed for more than a few moments. Ben showed me around and explained who he had as neighbours; on the one side he had a footballer and on the other some property owner. I knew that Donna, Becky and Danie lived here as well but again had never spent time visiting. I suddenly felt very guilty as they had always come to our house.

The estate looked really nice and Leigh had kept the gardening contract going looking after not only this estate but also the two others and was responsible for every conservatory base and orangery built, whereas Jake had been responsible for the production and erection of those items. Between the two of them, they had developed good solid and financially lucrative businesses.

Ben and I sat for the rest of the afternoon looking back at what we had achieved over the years and feeling that what we had done gave a great deal of job satisfaction. The next day the party at home started and the house was full. Julie had arranged for outside caterers to supply and serve the food and she had arranged for two cleaners to come after the party to tidy up; this way, Martha, Sally and Bridget could also relax and enjoy the day with us. The food was amazing and I could not believe the amount of drink we all got through, it was definitely a party to remember. I think it was the only time I ever saw Justin drunk, this showed that everyone was relaxed and enjoying themselves. At the end of the evening, I addressed the party by thanking everyone present on all levels for the outstanding contribution they had all shown over the years and their dedication to the company and family. I said that no man could have achieved what had been achieved without the support and guidance of those present, and although some parts were bigger than others, it all built this company and from the bottom of my heart, I thanked them all. We carried on drinking and laughing for hours after my little speech and I knew that the evening would be remembered for a very long time.

The next morning Julie and I were due to go to Donbecnie for a month but we were just too hungover to consider it. The house had been cleaned up by the two cleaners that Julie had arranged and the kitchen was tidy, but no one wanted food and like most people, the thought made us feel sick. All the bedrooms were occupied and people were sleeping on settees and in chairs, I had never seen this before here and I knew that everyone had had a brilliant night. The following day, Julie and I left our home behind and headed for Spain. We were planning on having a month to ourselves and making this the start of enjoying our retirement. I knew it would take some getting used to and I know that Julie had reservations that I could just sit back, but only time would tell.

Final Chapter

Demise

I am sorry to inform you that my husband and father to the girls, Donna, Becky and Danie died this morning in his sleep at the age of seventy-four. The doctor said he had a massive heart attack and would not have suffered. I am Julie, his wife for the past fifty-five years. I knew that he always wanted to write this book so that he hopefully would pass on any snippets of wisdom to anyone reading it. My husband had always dreamt of winning the lottery and doing what he had done in the past twenty-odd years. He had fulfilled his wishes and secured the future of all the family for generations to come. In the past couple of years, Jim had stepped back from the day-to-day running of the company and had hardly been involved other than attending the occasional board meeting, wanting to delegate responsibility to his loved ones. He had passed on the reins to Jonathan who was now C.E.O and myself as an Executive Director, Donna, Becky and Danie were Co-directors. To secure the direction of the company, he had insisted that any major decisions had to be made with a majority vote and if needed, I would carry the final decision in the event of a tie.

Prior to my husband's death, before he won the lottery, he worked as a self-employed gardener and garden fencer, fitting fencing and gates for anyone who needed it. He had built up the company from nothing and had made a comfortable living for many years. He made a conscious decision not to expand the business too far, as he was content keeping it as a one-man band. Winning the lottery changed his lifestyle and all of ours. From the outset, he became alive with determination to push the limits of all of us. He had a dream that he wanted a small empire to secure his family's future. It took him over twenty years of his life to fulfil his legacy and it will go on for many to come. He pushed all of us to become independent businessmen and women within our own rights and fulfil our potential. Jonathan had the head start on all of us with his private education and running part of his family's business for years. Looking back at some of the decisions my husband made at the time confused us all. With hindsight, he had made some excellent decisions that paid off big style. In the early days, he purchased and developed a centre of operations that had paid huge dividends. He had purchased as much land as he could and although none of us could quite understand why it become clear that this gave the company a grounding and secure income regardless of what happened in the rest of the company. He left the company financially secure with a very healthy bank balance and three daughters wealthy and competent in business.

My loving husband was cremated on the 22nd of August, 2023. Over two hundred people attended his funeral, including some of his best friends and of course all the family. The cremation took place in a crematorium some fifteen miles away and the chapel was packed. Outside it looked like hundreds of people had come to pay their last respects. The chapel had been decorated with some beautiful flowers mostly donated by the florist on estate one. Almost fifty people that were the closest to my husband came back to the house for the wake and I must say it was a dreadful but beautiful couple of hours; most people were in a state of shock and quite a few were close to tears throughout. I will miss my Jim and so will all the family, his drive and determination to look after his family's future was his final and singular goal in life.

God bless you, Jim, Love Julie, Donna, Becky and Danie, XXX

———————

Acknowledgements

I would like to thank all the people that have enabled me to produce this book and, although many of the characters are fictional, for allowing me to use some of the families' names in its story.

I would most of all like to thank my wife, Julie for being constantly at my side and pushing me to have it published as this was not my initial intention.

I would also like to thank my publishers, Michael Terence Publishing for their advice and dedication to bringing the manuscript to fruition.

Finally, I would like to thank Caroline Mylon for her patience and competence in editing my manuscript.

Thank you one and all.

Available worldwide online
and from all good bookstores

———————————

Michael Terence
Publishing

www.mtp.agency

www.facebook.com/mtp.agency

@mtp_agency

CPSIA information can be obtained
at www.ICGtesting.com
Printed in the USA
BVHW022249201122
652410BV00019B/587